Studies in the Out-Lying Fields of

by Hudson Tuttle

TO ALFRED E. GILES, OF HYDE PARK, MASS.,

AN ERUDITE SCHOLAR, A FEARLESS INVESTIGATOR, AN UNSHRINKING ADVOCATE OF HIS CONVICTIONS, HONEST AND TRUE TO HIMSELF AND OTHERS; IN RECOGNITION OF A MUTUAL FRIENDSHIP OF MANY YEARS THIS VOLUME IS FRATERNALLY DEDICATED.

ANALYSIS.

There is a Psychic Ether, related to thought, as the luminiferous ether is to light.

This may be regarded as the thought atmosphere of the universe. A thinking being in this atmosphere is a pulsating center of thought-waves, as a luminous body is of light.

There is a state of mind and body known as sensitive, or impressible, in which it receives impressions from other minds. This state may be normal, or induced by fatigue, disease, drugs, or arise in sleep. The facts of clairvoyance, trance, somnambulism and psychometry prove the existence of this ether, and are correlated to it.

Thought transference is also in evidence, as well as that vast series of facts which give intimation of an intelligence surviving the death of the physical body.

This sensitiveness may be exceedingly acute, and the individual unconscious of it, and then it is known as genius, which is acute susceptibility to the waves of the psychic atmosphere.

Sensitiveness explains the true philosophy of prayer.

All the so-called occult phenomena of mesmerism, trance, clairvoyance, mind reading, dreams, visions, thought transference, etc., are correlated to and explained by means of this psychic ether.

All these phenomena lead up to the consideration of immortality, which is a natural state, the birthright of every human being.

The body and spirit are originated and sustained together, and death is their final separation.

The problem of an immortal future, beginning in time, is solved by the resolution of forces at first acting in straight lines, through spirals reaching circles which, returning within themselves, become individualized and self-sustaining.

Spiritual beings must originate and be sustained by laws as fixed and unchanging as those which govern the physical world.

Sensitiveness gives great pleasures and may give pain; the author's experience as a sensitive, related, shows this.

And, finally, a communication from a spirit whose life had been noble and unselfish, given while the recipient was in a sensitive and receptive state, detailing an account of the phenomena called death, but which is really birth into the spirit realm, the meeting of friends, and the knowledge of a quarter of a century of its joys, together with "the poet's story," it being an account given by one whose earth-life had been selfish, and whose selfish thoughts had formed themselves into phantom companions, following him into the realm of the future world, and making his life there one of despair, and how he escaped these legitimate children of his brain by heroic acts of unselfishness, complete the story. These last are no fictions of the imagination, written to amuse the reader; but the author is firmly convinced, yes, knows they are the words of actual living beings who have once lived on earth like ourselves.

H. T.

CONTENTS.

Dedication

Analysis

CHAPTER I.

Matter, Life, Spirit

CHAPTER II.

What the Senses Teach of the World and the Doctrine of Evolution

CHAPTER III.

Scientific Methods of the Study of Man, and its Results

CHAPTER IV.

What is the Sensitive State

CHAPTER V.

Sensitive State: Its Division into Mesmeric, Somnambulic and Clairvoyant

CHAPTER VI.

Sensitiveness Proved by Psychometry

CHAPTER VII.

Sensitiveness During Sleep

CHAPTER VIII.

Dreams

CHAPTER IX.

Sensitiveness Induced by Disease

CHAPTER X.

Thought Transference

CHAPTER XI.

Intimations of an Intelligent Force

CHAPTER XII.

Effects of Physical Influences on the Sensitive

CHAPTER XIII.

Unconscious Sensitiveness

CHAPTER XIV.

Prayer in the Light of Sensitiveness and Thought Waves

CHAPTER XV.

Christian Science, Mind Cure, Faith Cure--their Physical Relations

CHAPTER XVI.

What the Immortal State Must Be

CHAPTER XVII.

Personal Experience--Intelligence from the Sphere of Light

Matter, Life, Spirit.

NECESSITY OF KNOWLEDGE, NOT FAITH.--Guizot forcibly expresses the value of a knowledge of future life when he says: "Belief in the supernatural (spiritual) is the special difficulty of our time; denial of it is the form of all assaults on Christianity, and acceptance of it lies at the root, not only of Christianity, but of all positive religion whatever."

He stands not alone in this conclusion. The difficulty, to a great majority of men of science and leaders of thought, appears insurmountable, and they no longer feel a necessity for defending their want of belief, but smile at the credulity of those who believe anything beyond what their senses reveal.

Not only the infidel world perceives this difficulty; it is well understood by the leaders of Christianity, for they have been taught its strength by the irrepressible conflict which has culminated in the want of belief at the present time. With this result before them, it is idle for the church leaders to assert that revelation in the Bible is sufficient to remove this difficulty, which has grown in the very sanctuary, in the shadow of biblical teachings. While the value of the Bible, as interpreted by theologians, depends on the belief in immortality, it has not proved the existence of man beyond the grave in such an absolute manner as to remove doubt; and yet, of all evidence it is designed to give, that on this point should be the most complete and irrefutable.

The resurrection of Jesus Christ proves nothing, even admitted in its most absolute form. If Christ was the Son of God and God himself, he was unlike ordinary mortals, and what is true of him is not necessarily so of them.

His physical resurrection does not prove theirs. Admitting similarity, his bodily resurrection after three days, while his body remained unchanged, does not prove theirs after they have become dust, and scattered through countless forms of life for a thousand ages. If, with some sects, the resurrection of the body be discarded, then the resurrection of Christ has no significance, for it is expressly held that his body was revivified and taken from the tomb.

Skepticism has increased, because the supporters of religion have not attempted to keep pace with the march of events, but, on the contrary, asserted that they had all knowledge possible to gain on this subject, and that anything outside of their interpretation was false.

Instead of founding religion on the constitution of man, and making immortality his birthright, they have regarded these as foreign to him, and only gained by the acceptance of certain doctrines. They removed immortality from the domain of accurate knowledge; and those who pursued science turned with disgust from a subject which ignored present research for past belief.

Hence, there has been, unfortunately, the great army of investigators and thinkers, in the realm of matter, studying its phenomena and laws, never approaching the threshold of the spiritual; and, on the other hand, the more important knowledge of spirit, of man's future, which retrospects his present life and all past ages, and reaches into the infinite ages to come, was the especial care of those who scorned nature and abhorred reason. Hence the antagonism, which can only be removed by the priest laying aside his books as infallible authority, discarding beliefs, dogmas, and metaphysical word legerdemain, and studying the inner world in the same manner that the outer has been so advantageously explored. When this has been done, it may be found that physical investigators have not the whole truth, even when they have been the most exact.

It may be found that, having omitted the spiritual side in all their investigations, their conclusions are erroneous to the extent of that factor, which may be one of the most important. It may be found that in order to have a complete and perfect knowledge of the external world, the internal or spiritual must be understood.

Here we face the time-old questions: What is matter? What is spirit? The philosophy of nature here rests. There is no middle ground. The materialist starts from the atom, which, he says, has in itself all the possibilities of the universe and outside of which there is nothing.

THE ATOM.--But who knows of the atom, into which matter, at last analysis, is resolved? No one. Aside from the active forces which apparently flow from it, we know nothing, and speculation takes the place of knowledge. That speculation, unfettered by the requirements of accurate science, grew rankly in the minds of the sages of antiquity, and bore the strangest fruits. From that time to the present, speculative thought has not ceased in activity, nor arrived at any certain conclusion.

The atomic theory is one of the most splendid generalizations in the whole circle of sciences. As a working hypothesis its aid is invaluable, and the solution it affords of the most intricate combination of the elements, truly marvelous. Yet it is a conjecture; the existence of the atom a guess. No one ever saw, tasted, or felt the atom. It is absolutely beyond the senses, as it is beyond any instrumental aid thereto. The entire structure of physical science, as expounded to-day, rests on conjecture, the only evidence in support of which is that it explains the phenomena. There is no assurance that other conjectures might not explain them quite as well.

It would be a waste of time to explore this field, wherein the baseless dreams of philosophers and scientists have grown like Jonah's gourd, overshadowing the barren sands.

The manner in which the nature of the distinct and indestructible atom was arrived at, shows the puerility of the theory. If we take a fragment of matter, we can break it into distinct pieces; these are again divided, and so on, until we reach a point where further division is impossible.

One of these indivisible particles, says the Materialist, is an atom; a conclusion derived from the gross conception of material division, and the limitation of the mind.

Endow this atom with force, or call it a center for the propagation of force, and the materialistic system is complete; yet these conclusions are but dreams. With equal arrogance, the Materialists lead to the higher ground of vitality, of mind and of morals, forgetting that the fundamental proposition on which this system rests is a guess, a surmise, and nothing more.

But investigation by other means than the primitive experience of mechanical division, shows that the atom has no existence as a fixed entity. Professor Crookes has demonstrated that matter has properties unknown to the present race of philosophers.

By way of illustration: If a certain vessel be closed, and the air exhausted, until only one hundred atoms remain, that hundred leave no space, but occupy the entire vessel. If the vacuum be made more perfect, and only ten atoms remain, the ten still occupy the whole space; and if the process could be carried so far that only one remained, it would still fill the space. The atomist might divide it indefinitely, and yet each division fill the space. In short, were there but one atom in the universe, that atom would fill all space.

NEW PROPERTIES.--When matter is thus rarified, or in other words, when the pressure is removed, new properties appear, and the tangible fades into the intangible. The qualities of pure force begin to be manifested. The intimation is made that were it possible to make the vacuum more perfect, there would arise out of this invisible gas, spontaneous manifestation of energy; or matter would be resolved into force.

WHAT IS MATTER?--Having seen that the conception of the atom is immature, and incapable of demonstration, we find matter, of which the atom is supposed to be the foundation, equally incapable of definition. With matter we never come in sensuous contact; we only know its forces, as expressed in phenomena.

The succession of seasons, the recurrence of day and night, the teeming earth, the starry heavens--these are manifestations of matter. Matter here is revealed to us as an appearance. Matter is appearance; phenomena are concrete expressions of force. It may be asked: Do these phenomena create themselves? Do bodies become organic by the confluence of atoms? Rather are they not molded by the force which through them gains expression? What is this force? Is it independent? On ultimate analyses, force resolves itself into motion, which is discernable to the senses only as expressed in phenomena. If we were obliged to explain the phenomena of matter only, some theory might be plausibly maintained; fronting one world we might understand it, but we are fronting two worlds. There is constantly the caused and the cause. We never are satisfied that the caused caused itself. We may receive the beautiful exposition of the doctrine of evolution, and yet we have only the road over which life has been irresistibly forced. Why? Wherefore? By what power? Instinctively we turn to the realm of spiritual causes.

Material science, with all its boasted accuracy and infallibility, breaks down, and utterly fails, when called to explain mental and spiritual phenomena. It boasts of infallibility, when its fundamental theories are conjectures that the advance of thought may to-morrow show to be vagaries of fancy. We must look to the eternal activities of spirit for the final solution of the grossest manifestation of matter.

NATURE A WITCHES' POT.--The present conception of nature, by material science, is a witches' pot, into which, by some unknown process, matter and force were placed. The pot seethes, and out of the seething conflict foams up to the surface in kaleidoscopic changes, organic beings. The savans stand around its rim like Shakespeare's witches and chant a technical gibberish about laws; the pre-existence and correlation of force; the indestructibility of energy; the eternity of matter; the potentialities of the atom; the struggle for existence; the survival of the fittest, and in admiration praise each other's profundity of sight, while the sharpest eyed see nothing beneath the foaming scum. They pride themselves on explanations, of causes, while really they play with words.

At the threshold of this discussion of the problem of mind and spirit we have that of life. The living being is the most wonderful achievement of force in its multitudinous forms. Life is the gateway to the realm of spirit, and beyond that gateway lie the questions we seek to solve.

The living being, by the fact of its being such, has new and hitherto undetermined relations. It has escaped from the hold of the forces in part from the common lot of matter, and a new horizon uplifts before it. New and mysterious forces intrude, the sum of which we call vital energy. Well we know that here the material scientist will smile or sneer, for he has already settled the question in his own mind and that of his confreres, that there is nothing beyond the properties of matter. The animal body is composed of definite quantities of carbon, hydrogen, lime, iron, etc., and the conflict of atoms, the combustion of carbon by the oxygen of the air, the burning of phosphorus in the nerves, is the activity evolved which is called life. In the higher animals, especially in man, this life force derived from burning elements is changed to thought, and the quantity of thought depends on the activity of the process.

No one, however, has ever proved that such transformation occurs, or even attempted the task. The most thoughtful and profound acknowledge that at the threshold of life all physical theories utterly fail, and that the problem does not admit of solution. The more persistent declare life to be a resultant of protoplasm; a fragment of protoplasm is the lowest form of a living being. It is a homogeneous mass, scarcely a cell or aggregation of cells. These cells do not feel or know; they are sensitive; that is all. A human being is said by these material scientists to be the sum of an infinite number of moners, as a coral branch is the sum of a great number of polyps. These moners form, under different circumstances, bone, muscle, and nerve. They propagate and die. Their multiplication and destruction is the source and accompaniment of vital changes, and mental states. When the necessity for the destruction of a great number of these moners arises, the end, the destruction of all, or death of the combined organism is the result.

According to this view, by the simple addition of moners, we obtain something none of them singly possessed. The single moner has only sensitiveness, their infinite aggregate, in the human being, has feeling, intelligence, will, and God-like aspirations. The time old axiom never before disputed is set aside, and the sum is declared to be not only greater than its parts--it is infinitely greater, and acquires qualities which the parts do not possess.

It may be urged that in the acquisition of new qualities the same is true of the chemical union of elements, which yield products entirely different in quality from the combining bodies. These, however, unite in fixed proportions in a manner far from understood, while, with the hypothetical moners, they are aggregated mechanically, as polyps in a cluster, and this union of individuals changes not their functions, but simply increases the mass.

Whether we accept this moner hypothesis, or the more generally received theory that life is the product of organization, arising from the chemical actions in the body, it is impossible to say wherein the dead animal differs from the living. Analysis can not reveal this secret, for the living animal can not be subjected to that test. The life principle escapes before the alembic or retort is brought into requisition. The song of the bird can not be found by chemical analysis. We know that the living being is held together, and dominated over by the strongest forces, and the moment these relax their hold, decomposition commences. What are these forces? Whence do they come? Whither do they go?

LIFE AND MIND.--Taking vital force in its highest expression, in man, it is self-conscious and has independent will. It arises above the atoms of its physical being, above the influences which environ it, and says, I will, and executes that will. I know well that if we here leave physical science for metaphysics, there are philosophers who would not only reason away this force, but the existence of the body itself. They are true intellectual acrobats; amusing jugglers, who throw words instead of painted balls, and confuse by their wonderful dexterity. Yet, after all has been said, we know we exist and have physical bodies. Had we not such bodies the thought of them would never have been fashioned in our minds. As we know the sun will rise, or the night follow, we know we have bodily forms, and are thereby brought in contact with the physical world. It is a fact, and as such can not be reasoned away. In the same manner we are conscious of a mental or spiritual life which arches the physical world as the dome of the sky.

IS THE GULF BETWEEN SPIRIT AND MATTER BRIDGED?--Here we come to that vague and uncertain realm where spirit touches matter. We leave the coast line of the tangible and seen for the intangible and unseen. There is no bridge over the gulf, which is said to be impassable. Material and spiritual phenomena are united by no common bond, and each stands by itself. The great thought stream has set toward the materialistic interpretation of all spiritual phenomena, or ruled them out of the pale of the believable. If these phenomena are real, if man--the ego--is superior to the oxygen and carbon of his body; if the manifestations of mind are superior to the combustion of tissue in the lungs, then all these manifestations should be amenable to certain laws and conditions, which ascertained, will harmonize them into a perfect system.

The brain is the point of contact between spirit and matter, and as far as the manifestations of that spirit are related to the material world while connected with the physical body, it must be through and by means of the brain. The intimate character of this relation gives strong color to the reasoning based on the material view that the brain produces thought, as the liver produces bile. But such reasoning is from appearance rather than the reality. There is, as Tyndall eloquently expresses, a chasm between matter and mind that can not be passed.

"The passage from the physics of the brain to the corresponding facts of consciousness is unthinkable.... Were our minds and senses so expanded, strengthened, and illuminated, as to enable us to see and feel the very molecules of the brain; were we capable of following all their motions, all their groupings, all their electric discharges, if such there be; and were we intimately acquainted with the corresponding states of thought and feeling,-- we should be as far as ever from the solution of the problem, 'How are these physical processes connected with the facts of consciousness?' The chasm between the two classes of phenomena would still be intellectually impossible."

SPIRITUAL SUBSTANCE.--As the experiments alluded to show that matter may, under certain conditions, take on new properties, ceasing to be matter, in the usual acceptance of that word, the horizon of matter which has been thought to rest over attenuated hydrogen, may extend to infinite reaches beyond, including stuffs or substances which have never been revealed to the senses. As the eye is capable of detecting only a narrow belt of rays, and the ear a scarcely broader belt of sounds, beyond which, on either side, are unknown realms of light and sounds, so we are able to detect only a narrow range of elements; and there may be a realm on one side too gross for recognizance by the senses, and on the other, one too attenuated. Beings fashioned of this attenuated substance might walk by our side unseen, nor cast a shadow in the noon-day sun.

SPIRIT ETHER.--Aside from this spiritual substance, beyond the pale of the most attenuated matter, is the spirit ether. The students of light have found it possible to explain its phenomena only by the hypothesis of an ether, a universal fluid of extreme tenuity, the vibrations of which are interpreted by the eye as light. This ether was at first a dream of the imagination; but, by answering all questions and receiving the verification of mathematics, it has become a demonstrated reality. It is probably the common medium for the transference of electricity, heat, and magnetism as well. It is an illustration of one of the many instances where the Imagination has overreached the Reason in the race of discovery.

In the same manner we may predicate another ether, the medium through which all spiritual phenomena are produced. We may prove the existence of this ether, by the certainty and harmony of the answers it gives, as the existence of the luminiferous ether has been demonstrated. As the great life-giver, we may distinguish it as psycho-ether. It can not be said to be material, for it belongs to the region beyond that recognized as material by our senses. It is the sublimation of matter, vastly more attenuated than light-ether, and thought is propagated in it from thinking centers, as light is in the luminiferous ether from luminous bodies. The qualities of this ether are the possibilities of life and spirit and to it for explanation we refer all psychic phenomena.

What the Senses Teach of the World and the Doctrine of Evolution.

IS THERE MORE THAN ONE WORLD--STUFF?--Thus far, with a few exceptions which may be called heterodox, physicists have in their speculations used the term matter as though in ultimate conception there is but one kind of matter and the atoms of that matter are absolutely alike. In other words there is but one stuff of which the cosmos is formed. The senses on which this theory is based do not endorse, but, by their limitation, prove the opposite. We have no means of knowing of sound aside from the ear, which is wonderfully fashioned to receive vibrations and transmit them to the brain; yet its imperfection, caused by the limitations of nerve tissue, reveals the fact that it is cognizant of only a narrow field, either side of which is a wide tract, which to it is profound silence. If a sound wave impinges on the ear with less vibrations than 16-1/2 times in a second it is inaudible; and if the number of vibrations is increased above 38,000 per second, they again lose the power of impressing the ear. There may be insects capable of hearing these high sounds, which to man are silence itself; and the long waves that beat less than 16-1/2 times in a second may be sweet music to some of the lower tribes of animated life.

Perfect as the eye may be as an optical instrument, its range is far less than that of the ear. Only those rays of light having waves 1-39,000th of an inch in length are visible on one side, and the last visible radiations on the other end of the spectrum have wave lengths of 1-575,000th of an inch. This is a narrow limit, and on either side there must be rays, which eyes or nerves differently constructed would receive and interpret, yielding, perhaps, colors unknown to our consciousness. There is a harmony in color waves, like music in sound waves, for as a note blends in one, in all octaves above or below, so light waves, twice or thrice the length of given waves yield the same color impression.

We may regard from the same point of view the sense of taste, the nerves of which have a still narrower range, and are apparently differently affected in animals than they are in man--substances disagreeable to him being relished by them, and of course affecting the taste differently.

We are not sure that there are not senses which appreciate conditions of matter, of which we have no conception. There are insects which apparently have organs bestowing senses unlike our own. Their antennae have no corresponding organs in the higher animals, and the conception of the world which these give has no analogy in our minds.

As the senses are thus cognizant of narrow belts of sound and light, leaving unknown stretches on either side, so what is called matter may be the narrow range recognized by our finite powers as a whole, on either side of which may lie stuffs of widely different qualities and possibilities.

A DEAD VIEW OF DEAD WORLDS.--Pausing to consider the received theory of force, as an explanation of the causes of the world--creation, we shall find that it fails to meet the high promises it vauntingly makes.

According to the received theory of force, every manifestation of power and energy on the earth is originally derived from the sun. The growth of plants and animals, and all the activities displayed by the latter, are derived from their food, which was produced by the light and heat of the sun.

In illustration of the sun's incalculable power, take, for instance, the rain fall of one-tenth of an inch extending over the United States. Such a rain-fall has been estimated at ten thousand millions of tons, which the heat of the sun had raised at least to the height of one mile. It would take all the pumping engines in the United States a century to lift this amount of water back again to the clouds. If the force is so great as displayed in the rain-fall of one-tenth of an inch, how incomprehensible the power which lifts the entire amount of water evaporated, amounting to, at least, forty inches!

Yet the force of the sun, manifested on the earth, is an inconceivably small part of that radiated, for the earth only receives in the proportion that its surface bears to the sphere of its orbit, and how incomparable is its diameter of 8,000 miles to that of a sphere 184,000,000 across. The combined surface of all the planets would receive a scarcely appreciable ratio of the entire amount which, unimpeded, flies away into the abyss of space.

The energy radiated at the surface of the sun is estimated at 7,000 horse power to the square foot, and if the sun was a mass of coal, it would have to be consumed in 5,000 years in order to supply it, and in 5,000 years would have to cool down to 9,000 degrees, C. If the nebular hypothesis be received, the contraction would supply the loss for 7,000 years before the temperature would fall 1 degree, C.

Incomprehensible as this force is, it is constantly diminishing, and although the projection of meteors and hypothetical cosmical bodies may prolong its action, the time must come when all its energy will be dissipated into space; all bodies will have the same temperature, and as there is no other source of energy, physical and vital phenomena will cease, and the universe, bereft of living beings, will itself be dead.

A DEAD WORLD.--According to the most advanced views at present entertained, this is the end of the career of the universe.

Balfour Stewart endorses this conclusion by saying: "We are induced to generalize still further, and regard not only our own system, but the whole material universe, when viewed with respect to serviceable energy, as essentially evanescent, and as embracing a succession of physical events which can not go on forever as they are."

In stronger language Mr. Pickering says: "The final result, therefore, would be that all bodies would assume the same temperature, there would be no further source of energy; physical phenomena would cease, and the physical universe would be dead. Such, at least, is the present view of this stupendous question."

In explanation of the origin of this energy, and the reason for its loss, Mr. Stewart further says: "It is supposed that these particles originally existed at a great distance from each other, and that, being endowed with force of gravitation, they have gradually come together; while in this process heat has been generated, just as if a stone were dropped from the top of a cliff toward the earth."

Thus the universe would become an equally heated mass, utterly worthless as far as the work of production is concerned, since such production depends on difference of temperature.

In other words, the universe becomes dead matter, wholly incapable of supporting life, and so far as present science gives us any information, must remain forever at rest.

The fact that such a conclusion has been reached should cause us to pause in doubt of the correctness of the data leading thereto. It would be more plausible were it shown how, at the end of the great cycle, there was renewal of the lost energy, and return to the nebulous beginning. Causation moves in cycles, and the most alarming perturbations are balanced by forces operating in other directions, so that the result is the preservation of order. Planets swing wide of their orbits for a million years, getting further and further away, yet the time comes when they return on a pathway carrying them as wide on the other side.

This latest view of the universe by scientific thought, however plausible its argument, or apparently logical its results, is proven by the very logic of those results to be defective.

THE LOGIC OF RESULTS.--It starts with the declaration that matter and force are inseparable, that there can be no matter without force. The nebulous beginning was a storehouse of energy, which has been wasting ever since the first world was formed. This force has been for countless ages dispersing by radiation. It is still wasting, for as it is radiated into space it does not even raise the temperature of the trackless abyss through which it passes. When it is all gone, there will be left the force of gravitation, holding with adamantine grasp the dead residuum of suns and planets; and, strange conclusion to which these premises force us, this residuum must be matter without force.

Here the problem remains unsolved, and a theory which proudly assumes for itself the distinction of being the only true system of nature, which rules God out of the universe, or makes Him an unknown and unknowable quantity, destroys life in nature, and has no means of its restoration except by a miracle. If the universe is a machine which in time will run down and die, all its force being dissipated, does it not follow that in the beginning some superior power united this force with matter? And also, does it not follow that if this dead universe again lives, a superior power must draw back the scattered beams of light, heat, magnetism, and other forces, and re-endow the dead residuum?

Thus this materialistic hypothesis, which boasts arrogantly of its certitude, begins in assumption and ends in a dilemma out of which confession of ignorance and acceptance of miracle only can extricate it.

Creation is not a clock that must be wound up at stated intervals by a foreign power, and any system which does not provide for its restoration as well as destruction, confesses weakness.

THE CHOICE OF CAUSES.--We have this choice: To believe that forces by blind action and reaction have evolved the world from a nebulous fire-cloud and peopled it with sentient and intellectual beings, making of it a perpetual motion, a machine not designed, but the result of infinite failures, perfected by infinite blunders, and sustained by the fortuitous equilibrium of unseeing, unknowing forces; or that back of these forces is an intelligence, planning and willing through their agency. If the latter be accepted, it does not follow that the crude conception of design in nature as the direct work of a personal God must be maintained. At the commencement of the great revival of the study of nature, when the views which have revolutionized scientific thought were beginning to dawn, illy defined and partially understood, they were seized on by a class seeking support to the theological doctrines they felt yielding beneath their feet, and distorted by plausible sophistry into apparent vindication of their dogmas. Of these, Paley became most famous, his illustration of the watch was the most renowned of his arguments. It is misleading, as there is no real likeness between a watch and the mechanism of nature. Yet we do not endorse the complacency of many leading supporters of evolution. Evolution is undoubtedly a true statement of the method of creation. It offers no further explanation and gives no cause. Accepting evolution and following the development of life from the least to the greatest, what do we see but the constant unfoldment of a well defined purpose and plan? Are not the beings of the Silurian and Devonian epoch prophecies of the forms which were evolved out of them? We may call things by new names, and in place of design use "adaptation"; we do not change the relations of things thereby. When we see a bird cleave the air with rapid wings, and observe the wonderful adaptation of bones and muscles and forms of feathers, we may explain it all by evolution, which has made the bird the embodiment of the forces of the air. Have we done more than state the method of growth? What cause have we assigned for the process? We see an interminable series of forms, changing from age to age, becoming more and more complex in their relations, but pressing forward constantly to final production of man as the perfection of the vertebrate type. Evolution describes this process, at every step furnishing evidence of a purpose, achieving its ends through matter, often failing, but through failures at last reaching its object. In this light the imperfection of organs proves nothing against design. The eye of man is instanced as more imperfect than a glass lens. It is as perfect as the organic material out of which it is made permits. That it becomes diseased is from the same necessity of organization.

EVOLUTION.--Evolution is a new name for facts exceedingly old; but its supporters would have its scheme reach through creation to the foundation of things. Advancement with them means only better adaptation in the struggle for existence, the result of accidental fitness which has pushed unorganized protoplasm to man. Matter and its potentialities granted, all else flows in assured course. Difficulties disappear; the riddle of the Sphinx is no longer obscure. The sunlight has fallen on the marble lips, and Memnon has revealed in a single sentence what mortal man has never understood, "The survival of the fittest." The theologian has rested in blissful confidence in the arms of the Creator; now comes the scientist who by easy methods calls the Creator "evolution," and falls as blindly confident into the arms of his new-named God. The likeness is made more complete by the scorn of one equaling the sneer of the other.

It is a new name for the old fact, that the forms of life on this earth are united by common parentage, and have been differentiated by the accumulation of infinite beneficial changes. The struggle for existence has been the center around which these have aggregated. This no careful student will deny. Having granted this, what then? Is anything explained? Have we approached the cause by a single step? Really, has anything been done more than to explain the phenomena of the world with new words and phrases?

Of old it was said the world is a machine with gods or a god at the crank; today the god at the crank is the Unknowable, the laws of nature, the potentiality of matter; or in the most recent theory the all-god has appeared in the revival of the god imminent in the universe, which is regarded as an organism, with a god-soul. This is poetic but neither sensible nor scientific. Forever and forever old ideas are washed on the shore of time, out of the wreck of the past, and instead for being relegated to the museum, are galvanized into grimace of life, and branded as new, when they are rapidly disintegrating in every part.

THE SURVIVAL OF THE FITTEST.--The survival of the fittest is a wonderful scheme of the preservation of the best. To illustrate, take the tiger and the deer. Once they herded together, the tiger not being, as now, noted for strength or cunning, nor the deer for caution and fleetness. The dull tiger was able to take as prey the least cautious and weakest of the deer. The fleetest deer propagated, and then only the most cunning tigers were able to procure food, and continue their kind. As their strength and cunning increased, the cautiousness and fleetness of the deer increased in this matched game of life; the two species reacting on each other until we now have the perfected deer and tiger. In both kingdoms of living beings, among all their diverse families and species, this struggle has gone on, and the result is the differentiation from abysmal protoplasmic slime the humming bird on the flower to the leviathan in the deep; the litchen on the rock to man with an intellectual comprehension of unknown breadth. We here have the chronicle of creation, and Froissart was not more garrulous with his exploits of lord and lady than the chroniclers of the changes effected in specific forms "on their way to man."

We hear all that is said, and with a feeling of disappointment, while admitting all, respond that we were promised a cause, and have been given only a method? What stands behind the "struggle for existence?" What is the infinite force of the ceaseless unrest, which throws each wave higher on the tide line, working like a blind giant, hewing out organic forms from protoplasm, and amid infinite failures approximating ever to the perfect, with constant prophecy that that perfection will be attained? The "survival of the fittest" reveals the prodigal method which preserves one of a million germs, casting the others back into the seething crucible for new trials. Can it claim anything more? The laws of nature are grooves in which causes run to effects; but why do they thus move? Calling them by other names will not satisfy. As Newton, when he gave the law of gravitation mathematical form, penetrated not a step toward its cause, so the biologist has not passed the threshold of the domain of life. A recent scientific association sat in silence after a verbose and flippant discussion on protoplasm, when asked by a member what was the difference between living and dead protoplasm? Not one could answer. Life had escaped their observation. Protoplasm dead is no longer protoplasm. The protoplasmic germ impelled by the forces of life, commences its growth, sending out its feeding vessels, and from the beginning copies the paleontological history of the earth, and more completely the biography of its direct ancestors.

When we consider that this invisible fleck bears in its cell or cells the impress of every condition bearing on its progenitors from remotest time, and will express it in all these conditions, it is no longer a phenomenon on which we gaze, but a miracle of creative power, and all that has been written by physiologists since Galen's time as to its cause is as children's prattle. The material side furnishes no adequate explanation. Its coarse methods are not adapted to measure the illusive psyche. The balance weighs not, the scalpel dissects not, the retort holds not the elements of the soul.

Scientific Methods of the Study of Man, and Results.

THE EVOLUTIONIST.--Scientists have different ways of studying man. The evolutionist first develops the form. He says that life began in protoplasm in the unrecorded ages of the past, and step by step, through mollusk, fish, saurian and mammal, has arisen by the "struggle for existence" and "survival of the fittest," until the mammal by strangely fortuitous chances has become a human being. As the human body is a modified animal form, so the intellect is a modified and developed instinct, the highest and most spiritual conscientiousness being only the result of accumulated experiences of what is for the best. The highest of animals is man, with no barrier between him and them, and subject to the same fate. There is no indication of a guiding intelligence, and if he possess an immortal spirit, so does the mollusk and the fleck of protoplasm.

THE CHEMIST.--The chemist has his method, that of analysis. He takes the vital tissues and resolves them into their elementary parts. He tells us that there is so much hydrogen, carbon and nitrogen in the muscles; so much lime and phosphorus in the bones; so much phosphorus in the nerves, and iron in the blood. He separates these elements in retort or crucible, and weighs them with nicety so that he knows to a thousandth of a grain their proportions. He has made the ultimate analysis, and these are all he can discover. Life is the result of their union; mind the burning of phosphorus in the brain, and as for spirit, it is quite unnecessary to explain the phenomena. The chemist has finished his work, and placed in the museum the results of his analysis. That body perhaps weighed one hundred and fifty pounds. In a large glass jar is the water it contained--clear, crystal water, such as flashes in the sunlight of a rainbow-arching shower, or a dewdrop sparkling on the petals of a lily. There are about eight or ten gallons of it, for the body is three-fourths water. There is a small jar of white powder representing the lime; another, still smaller, the silex; another the phosphorus. There are homeopathic vials containing a trace of sulphur, of iron, magnesia, the potash, the soda, the salts and so on until the vials, great and small, contain more or less of almost every element. Here we have what was once a human being. We have every thing that went to make him, except one, which lacking, these elements are lifeless, and of no more value than water from the brook and earth from its banks: the vital, or psychic principle. Place the contents of all the lesser jars in the greater water jar, shake, dissolve, and manipulate, dead and inert they remain, and will remain so long as thus treated. The chemist in his analysis has made no account of the subtile principle which made these elementary atoms an expression of its purpose. The living form has its origin in the remote past, and its atoms were arranged and brought into union by a vital process which thus began; which must begin in this manner and traverse the same path. Phosphorus may be essential to give activity to the brain, and a given amount of thought may correspond to a fixed amount of phosphorus burned in nerve tissue. What of that? We know that in one of these vials is all the phosphorus that existed in one human being; we may burn it all, and it will give flame, not intelligence. If intelligence comes from its burning, the process must take place in nerve cells organized for the purpose, and that structure must have been planned by superior thought.

To call the ingredients of these bottles a human being would be like calling a pile of brick, mortar and lumber a house, except the comparison fails in the house being built by outside forces, while the living being must be organized from within. No mixing of the contents of these bottles and jars can evolve life, or even the smallest speck of protoplasm.

THE ANATOMIST.--The third scheme is that of the anatomist, who with keen-edged scalpel bends over the body after life has gone out of it, and traces the course of arteries and veins, the form and location of nerves, the attachment of muscular fibers, and in connection with the physiologist defines the functions of each separate organ. An exquisitely fashioned machine it is, wonderfully and fearfully made, growing up from an invisible germ. After anatomist and physiologist have finished, and on their dissecting table only a mass of rubbish remains, they triumphantly point to it and exclaim: "See! We have settled the question of spirit! There can be nothing beyond this organism. We have determined how every cell and fiber of it are put together, and the functions they perform. No where is there an indication of any thing superior or transcending this material form. Here is where the food is digested; here it is assimilated; here this secretion is made; here excretion of poisonous matter takes place; here in the brain, in these gray cells, thought arises. Ah! it is a wonderful complex machine."

Indeed it is, and what has become of the power which moved it? You have a strange machine, unlike all others, for it is, according to your ideas, an engine to make steam, instead of to be moved by it; a mill to make a waterfall, instead of to be run by falling water. What is the difference between a dead man and a living one? Incomprehensibly great, and yet the dead man to the chemist, the anatomist, the biologist, is identically the same as the living. That unknown element, life, escapes the crucible, the retort, the scalpel, the microscope, and the conclusions of those who take it not into consideration are the vague conjecturing of children, who have gained but a half knowledge of the subjects that excite their attention.

Yet science proudly claims the knowledge of all things possible to know. It has searched into the foundations of the earth and ascended the starry dome of infinitude; it grasps the inconceivably small and the inconceivably great; it delves in the hard stratum of facts, and sports in the most sublime theories. It gives the laws of the dancing motes, and those which guide the movements of stellar worlds; the sullen forces of the elements and the subtle agencies which sustain living beings.

WHAT IS BEYOND THE STRIFE FOR EXISTENCE?--What, O Science, is there beyond the grave which shuts down with adamantine wall between this life and the future?

The answer comes: Beyond? There is nothing. Do not dream, but know the reality. What becomes of its music after the instrument is destroyed? Where is the hum of the bee after the insect has passed on its busy wings? Where is the light in the lamp after the oil is burned? Where is the heat of the grate after the coal has burned? Given the conditions and you have music, heat and light. When these conditions perish you have nothing. As the impinging of oxygen against carbon in the flame produces light and heat, so the combination of elements in the nerves and brain produces the phenomena of life and intelligence. As the liver secretes bile, so the brain produces thought. Destroy the brain and mind disappears, as the music when the instrument is broken.

Look you and see the strife for existence. See you the myriads of human beings who have perished. The world is one vast charnel house, its material being worked over and over again in endless cycle. Tooth and claw to rend and tear; arrow, club, spear, sword, and gun to kill; the weak to fall, the strong and brutal to triumph, to multiply, and advance by the slaughter of its own weaker members. The atom you can not see with unaided eye devours and is devoured, and ascending to man, he is by turns the slayer and the slain.

There's not an atom of the earth's thick crust, Of earth or rock, or metals' hardened rust, But has a myriad times been charged with life, And mingled in the vortex of its strife; And every grain has been a battle-field Where murder boldly rushed with sword and shield. Turn back the rocky pages of earth's lore, And every page is written o'er and o'er With wanton waste. The weak are for the strong, And Might is victor, whether right or wrong. Enameled armor and tesselated scale, With conic tooth that broke the flinty mail; The shell protecting and the jaw which ground The shell to dust, there side by side are found; The fin that sped the weak from danger's path, The stronger fin that sped the captor's wrath; A charnel house where, locked in endless strife, Cycle the balanced forces, Death and Life.

If you seek for a meaning or a purpose you will find none. What you call design is only the harmony of fluctuating chances produced by countless failures.

PHILOSOPHY.--Invoke philosophy with her robes of snow, pretending to a knowledge of the world and its infinite destiny; it will tell you of the cycle of being; the succession of generations; that life and death complement each other, and that all you may hope for is change. Unceasing change is the abiding law, and he who grasps to hold, will find but shadows in his grasp.

RELIGION.--Religion may teach us a pessimistic view of the world, and to bow like cringing slaves unquestioningly to the rod. We may accept that all is for the best whether we understand it or not, as the unalterable decree of fate, yet as rational beings we recoil from this bondage, and the questions are ever present, of the purpose of this life and the evidences of that future of which the most doubting dream.

Religion, resting as it does on the immortality of the spirit, should answer us so plainly and absolutely that there could be no doubt. That there is weeping and broken hearts shows that it does not, or else that it makes that existence so terrible that the dread of it is more than that of annihilation. The fear of Hell, which has driven the world to madness, is now cast into the lumber room with other errors, outgrown, and in the free atmosphere one can not understand the terrors it once awakened. The arbitrary heaven is also passing away, and a more natural conception of the future life is gaining precedent. Yet the words of teachers of religion are cold and soulless, and even the poets, touched by the finger of a decaying faith, voice the incredulity of the age in lines which speak only in despair. Oh! poet of immortal song, how chilling to the heart the words that yet too often find response in its doubts and fears:

"And the stately ships go on To their haven under the hill; But oh! for the touch of a vanished hand, And the sound of a voice that is still.

"Break, break, break, At the foot of thy crags, O sea! But the tender grace of a day that is dead, Will never come back to me."

There is little consolation to be found in these directions. Let us turn back to first principles; let us for a time forget the claims of scientists and take up the book of nature at her plain alphabet and ascertain whether these claims of material science have a sure foundation.

What is the Sensitive State?

A RACE WITHOUT SIGHT.--If the human race were born without organs of vision, man could form no idea of the beautiful and splendid phenomena revealed to the eye. The normal state would be blindness. Day and night would be marked by intervals of repose and activity, but the cloudy midnight and the radiance of the sun, the glories of morning, the splendors of sunset, the star-gemmed canopy of the cloudless night, the infinite changes, the phantasmagoria of heaven and earth, would be unknown. The flowers might bloom in beauty, their fragrance would delight, but their form and color would be unrecognized. The mind, deprived of the infinite series of sensations which flow into it through the sense of vision, would have none of the conceptions thereby engendered. If a being who could see should attempt to reveal to the sightless race the beauties of the world as seen by the eye in the light, they would treat him as an impostor relating an idle tale, to them incomprehensible.

A RACE WITHOUT HEARING.--If to the deprivation of sight were added the loss of hearing, the vital powers would not be impaired; the organic functions would continue the same, but all sounds would cease and perfect silence reign. The mind could form no conception of music, the songs of birds, the sighing of the wind, the roar of the storm, or the soft modulations of the human voice. As nature would be voiceless, so man would be dumb. The gift of speech would be lost with the power of receiving the sounds of words. The soul, in silence and darkness, unable to communicate its thoughts with others, would be bereft of all the sensations, emotions, and conceptions which arise from seeing and hearing, nor could it be taught these by those who possessed these senses, for no conceptions could be formed of sights never seen, or sounds never heard.

SENSITIVENESS.--In like manner, the sensitive condition reveals a universe which is unknown to the senses, and of which man is as profoundly ignorant as those born blind are of light. It is the heritage of all, yet manifested only at rare intervals in favored individuals. It is as it would be with the sense of sight, were thousands blind, while a few saw imperfectly, and only one with distinctness. The sight of that one would indicate what all might attain under favorable circumstances, as the perception of those who are sensitive shows what is possible in this direction. It is through this gateway that we are able to penetrate the arcana of a higher existence, and it is our purpose to go by easy steps along the pathway that leads into the vista stretching beyond this portal, into unexplored regions, of which scarcely a conception has yet been formed.

We have consciousness of spiritual realities, of an infinite after-life, and aspirations which it alone can satisfy, and for which this mortal sphere furnishes no provision. Shall we regard these aspirations as idle longings, and this consciousness as a baseless fancy? Or have we spiritual energies which have called this spiritual nature into being?

The eye is created in conformity to the laws of light, to receive the rays and allow their impingement on the optic nerves. It is proof of the existence of light. In the same manner, spiritual perception is evidence of the existence of spiritual energies. It would be quite as difficult for the mind to comprehend spiritual being, if without this consciousness, as for the blind to understand the beauties of light.

Sensitiveness is a faculty pertaining to the spiritual nature, and is acute in proportion as that spiritual nature dominates the physical senses. It is possessed by all, and by a few in a remarkable degree. It is variable in the same individual, is often the result of drugs, of fatigue, of sleep, and may be induced or intensified by hypnotism or mesmerism. It may manifest itself suddenly and at long intervals, once only in a lifetime, or be a steadfast quality. It may have all degrees of acuteness, from impressibility scarcely distinguishable from the individual's own thoughts, to the purest independent clairvoyance.

CONDITIONS AND ILLUSTRATIONS OF SENSITIVENESS.--For one mind to influence another, the two must be in harmony, at least in certain points. The thought vibrations in one will not otherwise awake like vibrations in the other. Take for illustration two musical strings, one with fixed attachments, and the other with a moveable bridge or stop. Now if the first be set in vibration, the other, being on a different key, will not respond in unison, but the stop will slightly move; and if the vibrations continue, the stop will move forward until the exact length of chord is attained, and then both strings will vibrate in harmony, one repeating the notes of the other.

If an hundred musical instruments were placed in a room, only two of which were tuned alike, if one of these were touched, its mate would respond, but the others would remain silent.

These thought vibrations may be received suddenly like a flash, as in the case of premonitions and warnings of danger, the sensitive state lasting but a brief time; or it may be cultivated and become permanent with the individual. The hypnotic, or somnambulic subject, may be more or less affected at first, and slowly fall under the influence, until the continuous condition is the same as that in which a premonition is received.

As an illustration of the method by which this is accomplished, whether the operator be a spirit clad in a physical or in a celestial body, the improvements by age and use of the violin may be taken.

This instrument, the most perfect of all in its capacity for expressing the delicate feelings of the soul, gains its soft sweetness and rich perfection by use and age. The cremona, worth its weight in gold, may once have been harsh, with dissonant tones, rasping to the ear. The Tyrolese maker selects the smoothest wood his mountain affords, clear of grain, and free from flaw or blemish. He carves the parts with sedulous care and exhaustless patience; swell and curve and hollow are wrought, polished, and cemented together so as to make them as one. Then the delicate strings are drawn over the bridge, and the instrument tested. It may squeak or jar, and refuse, even in a master's hands, to express his desire. But with every vibration of the strings it improves. Every movement changes its fibers, and forces them into harmonious accord. After a time they will all be in unison. The playing of a single tune may not produce this result; a score or a thousand may not. It may pass from hand to hand, and generation after generation may grow old and die, as each successive master touches its strings, before all its deepest qualities are expressed. Then its tones melt in voluptuous harmony; wail with the broken hearted; fill the soul with the gladness of delight; revive the murmur of the sombre pines; the song of the birds in the forest; the laughing of falling waters; the hoarse voice of the tempest with hail and lightning flash, rush of winds and burst of clouds. Nature speaks through the instrument, and vibrates the heart with every emotion, passion, and aspiration.

In the same manner, if a being independent of, and detached from the physical body, should attempt to impress its thoughts on a sensitive, it might no more than partially succeed after many trials. Each effort, however, would be more successful, for thought vibrations constantly tend to efface the causes of discord, and if the Intelligence is patient, and the sensitive submissive, the thoughts of the former would at last flow uninterruptedly into or through the mind of the latter.

And what is thus possible for a sensitive, in regard to an individual intelligence, is possible to acquire in relation to the thought atmosphere of the universe, or psychic-ether. If this be possible, if a being may become thus exquisitely sensitive, and receive the waves of thought as they traverse this ether, as the eye catches vibrations of light, that being would be a focus to receive the intelligence of all thinking beings in the universe.

The sensitive state, then, is the outcropping in mortal life, in apparently abnormal form, of that which is normal to the spirit of life. We thus conclude that its most astonishing development, as revealed, is immeasurably below its normal capabilities when freed from the limitation of the body. The permanent condition of a spiritual being after separation from the physical form must be that of the most perfect and delicately sensitive. What we see here in partial or total eclipse, is there in the glory of full light.

THOUGHTS NOT WORDS IMPRESSED.--While Max Muller ardently supports his theory that thought itself depends upon the words which express it, we constantly meet with facts which indicate that the idea is conveyed from one mind to another, and there is clothed in words according to the culture of the receiving mind. The vividness with which the idea is impressed insures the use of similar verbal clothing. An instance is reported by Dapson, in Deleuze, where a sealed letter was given a very susceptible magnetic subject. It reads:

"No other than the eye of Omnipotence can read this sentence in this envelope.

Troy, New York, Aug. 1837."

The subject read it:

"No other than the eye of Omnipotence can read this in this envelope. ---------- 1837."

He omitted "sentence," and all the date but the year. It is to be observed that in all instances of thought transference or sensitiveness, the reproduction of names, dates, etc., expressed by arbitrary words, are the most difficult and unreliable, and this has been a source of doubt, and an argument against the truthfulness of the magnetic subject.

It requires a deeper hypnotic state to receive dates and names correctly, than connected ideas. It is because ideas and not the verbal form are received, that culture becomes of greatest value connected with sensitiveness, as will be amplified in a succeeding section, treating on misconceived sensitiveness, whereby is made possible the seemingly superhuman achievements of authors, philosophers, sages, statesmen, and inventors. It will also be more extendedly treated of in the chapter devoted to the consideration of Dreams.

Sensitive State: Its Division into Mesmeric, Somnambulic, and Clairvoyant.

THE SIXTH SENSE.--In the normal state we know and understand the external world through and by the senses. The eye reveals to us the beauties of light, and by its aid the wondrous diversities of nature. The ear brings to the mind the varied sounds, makes oral speech and the sweet harmonies of music possible. The organ of smell sentinels the citadel of health against pestiferous odors, and gives the exquisite enjoyment of perfumes. Ordinarily we rely on these senses as our guides, and so complete is our reliance that we recognize no other avenue to knowledge of the external world; yet at times we find that our minds extend beyond the senses and have capabilities which can not be referred to them. There is an interior perception, which has been called the sixth sense, which, sensitive to impressions from supernal sources, at times rises above all the others. It is through this sense or better, this sensitive state, that we gain an insight into the spiritual nature of man. The senses would lead us away to a gross materialism, for they belong to the animal organization; this sensitiveness leads us in an opposite direction. We find through it another nature overlaid and obscured by the senses and their understanding. This sensitive state is the activity of the spiritual being, in the ratio of its perfection, and is really as normal as the most sensuous condition. The study of this state is the gateway to the understanding of our spiritual being, and the first lesson it teaches is that man is a dual creation; a spirit, an intelligent entity, clothed with, and circumscribed by, a physical body. Only so far as that body interferes with the activity of the spirit, is it of interest to us in the present discussion, which relates entirely to the spirit.

This sensitive state is possessed by many, and in many more it may be induced by proper means. It may be laid down as a rule that whatever weakens the physical faculties strengthens this spiritual perception. Thus it is often manifested in disease, after fatigue, or in the negative hours of sleep. Some drugs have the power of inducing it, and mesmerism is the strongest of all artificial means. I use the term sensitive with the meaning here given, and from that meaning shall not deviate. Many who possess this power in a slight degree may not distinguish its perceptions from those of the senses with which they blend, but there are times when the mind passes into an entirely different state from that of its normal activity, that of sensitive receptivity, and what is usually termed intuition is intensified. I propose to study this sensitive state first in connection with that of wakefulness, and then with that of sleep; and from simple thought-reading to the reception of thought from supernal sources.

Hitherto the discussion of spirit has been considered impracticable by scientific methods, and theology and metaphysics have occupied the field. In this border-land between the known and the unknown, ignorance and charlatanry have held high carnival, and those who love scientific accuracy perhaps are excusable in regarding the belief in spiritual beings as a superstition; yet there has accumulated as folk lore, as myths, as an outside, out-of-the-way literature, a vast mass of material, some of which, it is true, is mere rubbish, through which gleams bright veins of truth, showing the close relations between the seen and the unseen universes. Here and there a sensitive mind has received the light in clearer effulgence, and made the surrounding gloom more densely impenetrable. At remote intervals the oriflamme of the spiritual conception of nature has flashed athwart the intervals of gross materialism, but religion, moral conduct, not knowledge, has been the motive. This age demands knowledge for its own sweet sake, assured that the highest morality will flow therefrom. In the study of the conditions of the mind, the various states of sleep, clairvoyance, somnambulism, etc., will be defined and illustrated.

SLEEP.--Sleep is the "twin sister of death" only in appearance, for aside from poetic fancy, sleep is the negative condition of activity. In perfect sleep all the faculties of the mind are in repose, and the bodily functions go on with the least waste. It is essentially restful and recuperative. The waste of the body, its wear and tear of muscle and nerve is repaired; new cells take the place of those broken down, and the debris moves slowly forward to the excretory organs and is eliminated.

In this state of negative repose there is no manifestation of thought, and it is as unlike the clairvoyant or sensitive state as that of wakefulness; but shaded into this state of sleep, as into that of wakefulness, are various degrees of sensitiveness. The conditions of sleep are provocative of this impressibleness. Night is negative; the silence and the vail of darkness shutting out external objects conduce to make the mind negative and susceptible.

At midnight is the culmination of this negativeness, and hence the ghastly dread of that hour has a foundation in fact, and is not an idle superstition. Ghosts may never appear, yet if they were to appear the midnight hour, of all others, would be assigned by the student cognizant of this fact for them to come like shafts of frozen moonshine, into the walks of men.

MESMERIC STATE.--Mesmerism, under whatever name, animal magnetism, hypnotism, etc., is a potent means in the study of psychology. It has made it possible to command many of the most evanescent phenomena, and allow of their careful examination, when otherwise they came at rare intervals and at such unexpected moments as made it impossible to carefully compare and study them. Somnambulism, clairvoyance, and that state of exquisite sensitiveness which makes us receptive of impressions transformed into dreams, may be commanded in a sensitive, and observed at leisure.

In the commencement we must free ourselves from the commonly received idea that sleep has any resemblance to any of these several states which are usually called magnetic, mesmeric, or clairvoyant sleep. As already stated, sleep is the negative of being, and more distinct from these states of exalted perception than waking. The incongruous and often incoherent visions which arise in the half-waking state, or when only a part of the mental faculties are at rest, are the ordinary dreams, which have no significance, and are very different in their origin and meaning from the impressions received in the sensitive state, which is one of intense wakefulness and activity. The sensitive condition is possessed in a marked degree by about one in five, and may be induced in a still larger ratio. It is more frequently found in women than in men. It may be cultivated, and become an important factor in the character and happiness of the individual.

We will simply for convenience divide the sensitive state into the hypnotic, somnambulic and clairvoyant; but it must be borne in mind that these merge into each other; and that no sharp line can be drawn between them.

Mesmerism may be regarded as the method by which all of these states may be induced. The mesmeric state is equivalent to the hypnotic. After years of delay, mesmerism has been accepted under another name, that of hypnotism; but the theory of a "fluid" or specific influence is discarded. Hypnotists cannot, however, exceed the most common experiments without the facts demanding even as a working hypothesis, this specific influence.

The ticking of a watch held close to the ear, or intensely gazing at some object, will throw a sensitive into an abnormal condition, at the mercy of the "dominant idea," and he becomes an automaton in the hands of an external influence. This is the hypnotic state, beyond which the "dominant idea" fails. A sensitive may be led by a "dominant idea," but soon manifests a power which stretches beyond into an unexplored region of possibilities, exhibiting mental perceptions far more acute than those possess who are around him, or he himself possesses in his normal condition. Hypnotism as treated by its exponents is an extremely complicated state, ranging from the cataleptic to the independent clairvoyant. To define it with the usual narrow meaning is extremely misleading and unscientific.

There are two distinct states of hypnotism. The first is that in which most platform experiments are made. The sensitive is capable of carrying on conversations, answering questions, and is governed by a "dominant idea," believing all the operator wishes, and doing as commanded.

The sensitive rapidly enters the next stage, when he becomes insensible to pain, and irresponsive to the address of any one except the operator. Until this stage is reached consciousness and memory are retained, a fact fatal to the theory of automatic action or "unconscious cerebration." In this profound state the sensitive has no memory of events which occur. It is an induced, incipient somnambulism, the true counterpart of that which under proper condition appears spontaneously.

The report of the Committee on Hypnotism, vol. I., p. 95, of Proceedings of American Society for Psychical Research, shows that it confined its attention to fifty or sixty students of Harvard College. Of these about a dozen were affected, and of these, two were so good that attention was confined to them.

"The extraordinary mixture, in the hypnotic trance, of preternatural refinement of discrimination with the grossest insensibility, is one of the most remarkable features of the condition. A blank sheet of paper, with fine-cut edges, without watermarks or any thing which could lead to the recognition of one side or edge from the other, is shown to the subject with the statement that it is a photograph of a well-known face. As soon as he distinctly sees the photograph upon its surface, he is told that it will float off from the paper, make a voyage around the walls of the room, and then return to the paper again. During this imaginary performance, he sees it successfully on the various regions of the wall; but if the paper is meanwhile secretly turned over, and handed to him upside down, or with its under surface on top, he instantly recognizes the change, and seeing the portrait in the altered position of the paper, turns the latter about, 'to get the portrait right.'"

In the hypnotic state the subject is under the control of the operator, and in a great degree an automaton; in the somnambulic, he in part regains his individuality, and in certain lines of thought and action is superior to himself in his waking moments. Natural somnambulism comes without warning, and illustrates the condition induced by mesmeric passes.

SOMNAMBULISM.--Sleep waking, or sleep walking, whatever may be its cause, mental derangement by disease or intense exertion of mind or body, or a constitutional inclination thereto, is of deepest interest to the psychologist as proving the independence of the spirit of the physical senses. The somnambulist has lost the use of his senses. He feels, hears and sees nothing by touch, ear or eye, and yet the objects to which his attention is drawn are plainly perceptible.

The Archbishop of Bordeaux is authority for the following narrative: A young clergyman was in the habit of rising from his bed, and writing his sermons while asleep. When he had written a page he would read it aloud and correct it. Once in altering the expression "ce devin enfant," he substituted the word "adorable" for "devin," which, commencing with a vowel, required that "ce" before it should be changed to "cet;" he accordingly added the "t." While he was writing the Archbishop held a piece of pasteboard under his chin to prevent him seeing what he was writing, but he went on without being in the least incommoded. The paper on which he was writing was removed and another piece substituted, but he at once perceived the change. He also wrote pieces of music with his eyes closed. He once wrote the words under the notes too large, but discovering his mistake, he erased and rewrote them. He certainly did not see with his eyes and yet the vision was perfect.

The case of Jane C. Rider, known as the Springfield somnambulist, created in its time much wonder and speculation among intelligent persons acquainted with the facts. A full account of it was published in the Boston Medical and Surgical Journal, Volume XI., Numbers 4 and 5. Miss Rider would walk in her sleep, attend to domestic duties in the dark or with her eyes bandaged, and read in a dark room with her eyes covered with cotton batting, over which was tied a black silk handkerchief. She learned without difficulty to play at backgammon while in this state, and would generally beat her antagonist, though in her normal state she knew nothing about the game.

A young lady, while at school, succeeded in her Latin exercises without devoting much time or attention to them, apparently. At length the secret of her easy progress was discovered. She was observed to leave her room at night, take her class-book, and go to a certain place on the banks of a small stream, where she remained but a short time and then returned to the house. In the morning she was invariably unconscious of what had occurred during the night; but a glance at the lesson of the day usually resulted in the discovery that it was already quite familiar to her.

A young man on a farm in Australia, after a hard day's work, went to sleep on a sofa; after some little time he arose, passed through several gates, opening and fastening them. Reaching the shed, he took off his coat, sharpened his shears, caught a sheep, and had just finished shearing it when his companions came with lanterns in search of him. The shock of awaking caused him to tremble like a leaf, but he soon recovered. The sheep was shorn as perfectly as if the work had been done in broad daylight.

MORAL EFFECT OF MESMERISM.--Dr. Voisin recommends a suggestive application of mesmerism. He experimented on a coarse, debauched and lazy woman, who was susceptible to magnetism; and kept her in the mesmeric sleep ten or twelve hours a day, and to its value as a curative agent he added moral education. During her sleep he suggested ideas of obedience, of submission, of decency, and exhorted her to useful labor. In this sleep she memorized whole pages of moral books. A complete transformation was effected in her in a few months.

What a glorious field here opens for the moral reformer! The calloused criminal who will not listen to moral suasion, deaf alike to entreaty and prayer, may be hypnotized, and in that susceptible condition taught the Lord's Prayer and moral precepts; his moral nature roused and thus be transformed into a new being. The influence of some men when brought into contact with criminals is explained by their strong mesmeric or hypnotic influence. They always lift up those they control. They are born masters, though they may not understand the cause of their strength.

TRANCE AND CLAIRVOYANCE.--The trance or clairvoyant state has been observed in all ages and among all races of mankind. It has, in seasons of great religious excitement, become epidemic, the devotee falling in convulsions, becoming cataleptic, and after hours, days, or even months of apparent death, awakening with mind overwrought with visions of the strange world in which it had dwelt during the period of unconsciousness.

The records of clairvoyance are as old as history. If prophecy, the "clear seeing of the future," be its fruit, the prophets and sages of the past were all more or less endowed with this gift. Socrates and Apollonius predicted, and were conscious of, events transpiring at remote distances. Cicero mentions that when the revelations are being given, someone must be present to record them, as "these sleepers do not retain any recollection of them." Pliny, speaking of the celebrated Hermotimus, of Clazomenae, remarks that his soul separated itself from the body, and wandered in various parts of the earth, relating events occurring in distant places. During the period of inspiration his body was insensible. The day of the battle of Pharsalia, Cornelius, a priest of profound piety, described while in Padua, as though present, every feature of the fight. Nicephorus says that when the unfortunate Valens, taking refuge in a barn, was burned by the Goths, a hermit named Paul, in a fit of ecstasy, cried out to those who were with him: "It is now that Valens burns." Tertulian describes two females, celebrated for their piety and ecstasy, that they entered that state in the midst of the congregation, revealed celestial secrets, and knew the innermost hearts of persons.

St. Justin affirms that the sibyls foretold events correctly, and quotes Plato as coinciding with him in that view. St. Athenagoras says of the faculty of prescience, that "it is proper to the soul." Volumes might be readily filled with quotations like the foregoing, showing that clairvoyance has been received as true by profound thinkers in every age. Swedenborg, Zschokke, Davis, are not peculiarities of modern times, but repetitions of Socrates, Apollonius, and countless others who deeply impressed their personality on their times.

WHAT IS CLAIRVOYANCE?--Clairvoyance is a peculiar state of impressibility, presenting gradations from semi-consciousness to profound and death-like trance. Whether natural, or induced by artificial means, the attending phenomena are similar. In its most perfect form the body is in deepest sleep. A flame may be applied to it without producing the quiver of a nerve; the most pungent substances have no effect on the nostrils; pins or needles thrust into the most sensitive part give no pain; surgical operations may be performed without being felt. Hearing, tasting, smelling, feeling, as well as seeing, are seemingly independent of the physical organs. The muscular system is either relaxed or rigid; the circulation impeded in some cases until the pulse becomes imperceptible; and respiration leaves no stain on a mirror held over the nostrils.

In passing into this state, the extremities become cold, the brain congested, the vital powers sink, a dreamy unconsciousness steals over the faculties of the mind. There is a sensation of sinking or floating. After a time the perceptions become intensified; we can not say the senses are intensified, for they are of the body, which for the time, is insensible.

The mind sees without the physical organs of vision, hears without the organs of hearing, and feeling becomes a refined consciousness, which brings it en rapport with the intelligence of the world. The more death-like the conditions of the body, the more lucid the mind, which for the time owes it no fealty.

If, as there is every reason to believe, clairvoyance depends on the unfolding of the spirit's perception, then the extent of that unfolding marks the degree of its perfection. However great or small this may be, the state itself is the same, differing only in degree, whether observed in the Pythian or Delphic oracle, the visions of St. John, the trance of Mohammed, the epidemic catalepsy of religious revivals, or the illumination of Swedenborg. The revelations made have a general resemblance, but they are so colored by surrounding circumstances that they are extremely fallible. The tendency of the trance is to make objective the subjective ideas acquired by education. This is exhibited in cases of religious ecstasy and trance, when the subject sees visions of winged angels and of Christ; transforming dogmas and beliefs into objective realities. Such revelations, of course, have no more value than the illusory visions of the fever-stricken patient.

Yet there is a profound state which sets this aside, and divests the mind of all trammels, and brings it into direct contact with the thought atmosphere of the world--the psycho-ether. Time and space for it, then, have no existence, and matter is transparent.

The weakening of the physical powers by disease is favorable to sensitiveness. As the senses are deadened, the powers of the interior consciousness are quickened, and a new world rises above the horizon of the corporeal senses.

Evidence of the truth of clairvoyance was given in the Brooklyn Eagle, soon after the loss of the "Arctic," in 1854. The wife, son and daughter of Captain Collins were making the tour of Europe, and the Captain, to gratify a passing whim, consulted a clairvoyant as to their locality. The answer was that they were at that time visiting a church, which was accurately described. When the wife's letter came, it contained a narrative of a visit to a church at exactly the same hour, describing it as the clairvoyant had done, thus showing that the communication was quite correct.

As the family had arranged to return on the "Arctic," and as the ship was a day late, of course Captain Collins became anxious. Sunday and Monday passed without news from the ship, and his anxiety increased. He thought of the clairvoyant and called on her. At first, although apparently deeply entranced, she could see nothing. Everything was in a cloud. At length she was able to see the three persons standing on the deck of a ship, amid great confusion, and almost concealed in fog and mist. This was all she could discern. This was nearly two days before the telegraph announced the loss of the "Arctic," and the arrival of a boat-load of survivors on the Canadian coast. But the Collins family were not among the saved.

If we compare what may be called artificially induced with the spontaneous clairvoyance, we shall find them similar. The first example is of a sensitive, a youth of seventeen, who was blindfolded by means of soft paper folded double, and then gummed over his eyelids, and a silk handkerchief tied over this paper. Under these circumstances the sensitive was able to take a pack of cards and select any one called for, read the pages of a book, although those present were ignorant of the words, his sensitiveness being entirely independent of the knowledge of those around him.

CLAIRVOYANCE FROM DISEASE.--There are instances where persons have fallen into this sensitive or clairvoyant state by disease or a nervous shock, and in the prolonged trance which followed, manifested all the phenomena usual to the induced somnambulic or clairvoyant state, even in higher degree. Of these Mollie Fancher is one of the best examples. She was called the "sleepless girl of Brooklyn," and for nine years, it is claimed by competent authority, did not sleep, and ate so little food that it was claimed she did not partake of any. She was, at fifteen years of age, healthy, but delicately organized. At that time she was thrown from a street car, and her head and body injured. A day or two afterwards she was seized with violent spasms. One by one her senses failed. Sight was first to leave, and hearing followed. Then she lost her speech, and then the ability to swallow. This last she had not been known to exercise for nine years, and during the same length of time her eyelids were closed. She took no sleep, unless the intervals of trance be called sleep. She was breathless and rigid as dead. These spasms lasted less than a minute, and were accompanied with, or followed by, violent muscular contortions.

Her lower limbs became twisted entirely around each other. Her right arm was bent upward and doubled under her head. She had no use of her right hand at all, and of the left hand only the thumb and little finger. Lying all the time, night and day, upon her right side, her right hand cramped under her neck, and only her left free, with closed eyes, and working back of her head, as she was forced to do, she wrought the most exquisite worsted work and wax flowers. The darkness or light were all the same to her; in fact, the light was painful to her, and even the gas-light was placed in the further corner of the room and shaded. She regained hearing and speech after several years, but otherwise her conditions remained unchanged. She knew the thoughts of those who came near her; printed pages or a sealed letter held in her hand back of her head were readily read. Mr. Henry Parkhurst made many experiments to test her powers. She repeatedly read sealed letters he gave her, and, as a crucial test, he took a letter at random from the waste basket of an acquaintance, tore it in strips, and then cut the stripes into squares. He shook the pieces well together, put them into an envelope, and sealed it. This he handed the blind girl. She passed her hand over it several times, took a pencil and wrote the letter verbatim. Mr. Parkhurst opened the envelope, arranged the pieces, and found she had made a perfect copy.

Not satisfied, with the assistance of two friends, Mr. Parkhurst secured an ancient mining report, yellow with age, and with averted face, so that he might not see the contents, he tore out a page of tabulated figures with explanation. This he folded and tore into scores of pieces. Some of the pieces fell on the floor and were allowed to remain there. The others he put in an envelope and sealed, and handed to one of his assistants, who put it in another envelope, which he also sealed and handed to the third, who enclosed it in the same manner. Then the party went to Miss Fancher's room, and asked her to give them the contents of the envelope. She took it in her hand and wrote, "It is nonsense; figures in which there are blank places, words that are incomplete, and sentences in which words are missing." She wrote on, in some sentences skipping three or four words, and began with the last five letters of a word having ten letters. The table of figures she made contained blank spaces, but she wrote it out; and the gentleman returned to Mr. Parkhurst's, where they arranged the pieces in their original form. They found that the copy made by Miss Fancier was absolutely correct, and the blank spaces represented the pieces left on the floor. When these were fitted in, the broken sentences were complete.

Dr. Spier, from the first her attending physician, watched her case with unrelenting vigilance, and made a full record of her changing symptoms. One day he received a note from her, warning him that an attempt would be made to rob him, and the next day the attempt was made. She knew when he was coming, and would mention the moment he started from his residence, a mile away. In the early stages of her illness, Dr. Spier administered an emetic to test whether the claim that she had not partaken of food was true. It gave her great pain, and proved that her stomach was empty. She well knew the nature of the medicine, although purposely he attempted to keep it from her. Soon after she went into the rigid condition which lasted nine years. When she began to recover, the memory of these nine years was gone, and she only remembered the incidents of the previous. Nine years and a half after administering the test, when Dr. Spier entered the room, Miss Fancher broke out with: "You thought I didn't know you gave me that medicine, but I did. You wanted to learn if food was in my stomach, but found none there. It made me very sick. You will not do so again, will you?"

Thus she returned after all that time to the thought which she had at the moment of entering on that strange experience. She had a double life, and did not remember anything which occurred in her trance.

A SIMILAR CASE IN ENGLAND.--The case of Mollie Fancher is not alone, although, perhaps, not more remarkable than that of Miss Eliza Hamilton of England. A physician visited her in 1882, when she was fourteen years of age. He found that in 1881 she had met with a severe injury which had caused paralysis of her limbs and right arm. She had been treated at the hospital for four months, at the end of which time she ceased to take food and returned home. He saw her about two months thereafter, and thus speaks of her: "She frequently passes into a trance condition, in which her left arm becomes as stiff and immovable as her right one. She sings hymns and repeats passages from the Bible, but is quite insensible to pain when pinched or pricked with a pin; nor does she hear or speak when addressed. When she revives, she tells her friends that she has been to various places and seen various people, and describes conversations which she has had, and objects she has seen in the rooms of persons she has been visiting. These descriptions, on inquiry, are found to be correct.... At times she speaks of having been in the company of persons with whom she was acquainted in this world, but who have passed away; and she tells her friends that they have become much more beautiful, and have cut off the infirmities with which they were afflicted while here. She often describes events which are about to happen to her and are always fulfilled exactly as she predicts."

Her father read in her presence a letter he had received from a friend in Leeds, speaking of the loss of his daughter, about whose fate he and his family were very unhappy, as she had disappeared nearly a month before and left no trace. Eliza went into the trance state, and cried out, "Rejoice! I have found the lost girl! She is happy in the angel world." She said the girl had fallen into dark water where dyers washed their cloths; that her friends could not have found her had they sought her there, but now the body had floated a few miles and could be found in the River Aire. The body was found as described.

Now, knowing that her eyes were closed, that she could not hear, that her bodily senses were in profound lethargy, how are we to account for the intensivity and keenness of sight, the quick deftness of figures enabling her to make the most beautiful contrast of colors in her worsteds, or the delicate adjustment of the petals of her flowers? Her mental powers were exceedingly exalted, and scarcely a question could be asked her but she correctly answered.

In this case the independence of the mind of the physical body shown in every instance of clairvoyance, is proven beyond cavil or doubt. If it is demonstrated that the mind sees without the aid of eyes, hears when the ears are deaf, feels when the nerves of sensation are at rest, it follows that it is independent of these outward avenues, and has other channels of communication with the external world essentially its own.

It must be here observed that as long as the mind is united with the body, usually the physical senses overlay and conceal the higher psychic faculties. The mind seemingly is dependent on the body, and is changeful to corporeal conditions. It becomes enfeebled by disease, by accidents to the brain, and at times disappears, like a lingering spark from a flame, in the dotage of age. This, however, is only external appearance, arising from the limitations fixed by the contact with physical matter, as the light of the sun may be shut out by an opaque body.

The case of Laura Bridgeman is an illustration and evidence from another point of view that the intellect is, in a measure at least, independent of the senses. Completely deprived of sight and hearing at an early period of childhood, she was a blind and deaf mute. She never had any knowledge, through the eyes, of the bright landscape, of the glorious sun, morning and evening, the blue sky, the floating clouds, the waving trees, the green hills, the beautiful flowers. All was darkness and profound night. She never heard the exquisite notes of harmony, of instrument or modulated voice, the sigh of winds, the carol of birds. To her all had been unbroken silence. Dr. Howe, her kind and angelic teacher, says: "As soon as she could walk she began to explore the rooms of the house. She became familiar with forms, density, weight, and heat, of every article she could lay her hands upon.... An attempt was made to give her knowledge of arbitrary signs by which she could interchange thoughts with others. There was one of two ways to be adopted: Either to go on and build up a language of signs which she had already commenced herself, or to teach her the purely arbitrary language in common use; that is, to give her a sign for every individual thing, or to give her a knowledge of letters, by combinations by which she could express her ideas of the existence, and the mode and condition of existence of anything. The former would have been easy, but very ineffectual; the latter seemed difficult, but if accomplished, very effectual. I determined, therefore, to try the latter."

After describing the process by which he taught her to associate names with things, he goes on to say; "Hitherto the process had been mechanical, and the success about as great as teaching a knowing dog a variety of tricks. The poor child had sat in mute amazement, and patiently imitated everything her teacher did. But now the truth began to flash upon her; her intellect began to work; she perceived that here was a way by which she could herself make up a sign of anything that was in her mind, and show it to another mind, and at once her countenance lighted up with a human expression. It was no longer a dog or a parrot; it was an immortal soul, eagerly seizing upon a link of union with other spirits! I could almost fix upon the moment the truth first dawned upon her mind, and spread its light to her countenance. I saw that the great obstacle was overcome, and henceforth nothing but patient perseverance, and plain, straight-forward efforts were to be used."

At the end of the year, a report of the case was made, from which the following extract is taken: "It has been ascertained beyond a possibility of a doubt, that she can not see a ray of light, can not hear the least sound, and never exercises her sense of smell if she has any. Thus her mind dwells in darkness and stillness, as profound as that of a closed tomb at midnight. Of beautiful sights, sweet sounds, and pleasant odors, she has no perception; nevertheless, she is happy and playful as a lamb, a bird, and the enjoyment of her intellectual faculties, or the acquirement of a new idea, gives her a vivid pleasure, which is plainly marked in her expressive features.... In her intellectual character, it was pleasing to observe an insatiable thirst for knowledge and a quick perception of the relation of things. In her moral character, it is beautiful to behold her continued goodness, her keen enjoyment of existence, her expansive love, her unhesitating confidence, her sympathy with suffering, her conscientiousness, truthfulness and hopefulness."

Her spirit was locked within her body without the least contact with the world through the most useful senses; yet she not only thought, but thought in the same manner as those who possess these senses in perfection. If thought depends on the senses, then the quality of thought should change when deprived of the senses. It is true that when thus fettered in expression, it does not escape the limitations of its surroundings, yet in the struggle we see the indication of the limitless possibilities of the spirit when these are cast aside.

Sensitiveness Proved by Psychometry.

Light emanating from suns and worlds, as it wings its swift way across the regions of space, bears on its rays the pictures of every object from which it is emptied or reflected, and hence the universe, from center to remotest bounds, is filled with pictures; is a vast storehouse of photographs of all events from the fading of a leaf to the revolution of a world since time began. Thus a ray of light leaving the earth during the coal age bears a picture of the then existing gigantic forests and inky seas, and is yet somewhere passing the remote coastlines of unknown systems, and could some swifter messenger overtake it, he would have a view of the world as it was when that ray was reflected from the carboniferous period. The messenger is not needed to overtake the fugitive ray, for the light thus reflected, struck against rock and tree, and photographed the images of every moment since the stars first sang together. Every atom still vibrates to the molding hand of life under which it has at some time passed, and the sensitive mind is able to catch these vibrations and interpret their meaning in forms of thought. The discovery of this wonderful faculty of the mind is not of recent date.

Almost fifty years ago an Episcopal Bishop remarked to Dr. Buchanan that when he touched brass, even in the night, when he could not know with what substance he came in contact, he at once felt a disagreeable influence and recognized an offensive metallic taste. Such experience had been common to a great number of persons, and frequently observed, but this time it was called to the attention of the right man. All the world for ages had seen bodies fall to the ground, and countless millions of eyes have seen the phenomenon with no more thought than the brute, until a falling apple drew the attention of Newton. Dr. Buchanan at once saw that there was a profound philosophy back of this fact which transcended the senses. He began a lengthy series of experiments, by which he discovered that it was by no means rare for persons to be affected by metallic and other substances. In a class of one hundred and thirty students at the Eclectic Medical College, forty-three were sensitive in greater or less degree. Medicines held in the hand without any knowledge of their properties, produced the same effect, varying only in degree as when taken into the stomach. By placing the hand, or merely coming into the atmosphere of a deceased person, the sensitive was able to locate and describe the disease. In this field Dr. Buchanan has stood almost alone, until recently M. Bourru and M. Burot of the Naval Medical School at Rochfort, have made extended experiments on the "action of medicines at a distance," which is really another way of stating the facts observed by him a generation ago. They held the metals and drugs six inches or so from the back of the head of the patients and proved all that Dr. Buchanan claimed for his discovery.

But the discoverer did not rest here; he went a step further and found that a letter or any article having been brought in contact with the person, when taken in the hand or placed on the forehead of one sufficiently sensitive, gave the character of its writer or owner. Repeated experiments, such as any one may make, prove beyond question that the sensitive can in this manner read the character of the writer from his writings, his state of health, better than the most intimate friend, or even the writer himself. It is a marvelous statement, but only marvelous in our not understanding its cause. When this is revealed, and mystery removed, the subject allies itself with other phenomena of mind, having their origin in impressibility.

Prof. Denton carried the results of psychometry far beyond the boundaries reached by Dr. Buchanan. If the world is one vast picture gallery of every act and thought since the beginning of time, the fossil shell, the rock-fragment, the broken arrow head, the shred of mummy, and the rush leaf from the banks of the Nile should reproduce in the sensitive the story of their origin and age. By a great number of experiments, the details of which fill three volumes, Prof. Denton sought to establish this generalization and write the geological and pre-historic history of the earth. That he found a kernel of truth can not be denied, but he allowed sources of error to creep in and vitiate his wonderfully suggestive and patient research. A person sensitive to the degree that enables him to feel the influences given to a fragment of stone thousands of years ago, would be more strongly impressed with the influence imparted by the one who secured it, and held it in his hands before the experiment. It is from this cause that uncertainty rests on his otherwise well-planned experiments. Yet he has proved that such sensitiveness exists, and that by it the story of history from fragments of ruined architecture may be read, and scenes in geological ages by fossil, bone or shell be described.

How? Really psychometry, depending on the sensitiveness of the brain, is a lower degree of clairvoyance, and is merged, in its clearest forms, therein. Sensitiveness means the capability of receiving the psycho-ether waves as they pulsate from some center, and as everything touched by life is in a state of such vibration, the recognition is only a question of the delicacy of the receiving organization.

There is a vast accumulation of narratives of ghosts, witches, apparitions, hallucinations, illusions, dreams, etc., which it is the present fashion to relegate to the sphere of superstition and ignorance. Many of these, however anomalous, have a foundation in fact, and will be found, when stripped of the portions superstition has added, readily explainable, either as subjective, arising from impressions on the sensitive, or as objective and manifested by the same principles. As sensitiveness to these subtle influences greatly varies in different individuals and at different times in the same individual, and at times becomes clairvoyance, scarcely an illustration can be given of one without introducing the other. We must constantly bear in mind that there is one fundamental cause back of all these so-called occult phenomena, varying in the degree of its manifestation in accord with the channel through which it flows.

SUBJECTIVE SPECTRAL ILLUSIONS.--Dr. Abercrombie is authority for the following illustration of subjective spectral illusions: "A gentleman of high mental endowments, and now upwards of eighty years of age, of spare habits and enjoying uninterrupted health, has been for eleven years subject to the daily visits of spectral figures. They in general present human countenances; the head and body are distinctly defined, the lower parts are for the most part, lost in a kind of cloud. The figures are various, but he recognizes the same countenances repeated from time to time, especially of late years, that of an elderly woman, with a peculiarly arch and playful expression, and a dazzling brilliancy of eye, who seems just ready to speak with him.... This female is dressed in an old-fashioned Scottish plaid of Tartan, drawn up and brought forward over the head, and then crossed below the chin, as the plaid was worn by aged women in his younger day. He can seldom recognize among the spectres any figure or countenance which he remembers to have seen; but his own face has been presented to him, gradually undergoing the change from youth to manhood, and from manhood to old age."

It is not necessary to call in the aid of an invisible being to explain such appearances. The house had been occupied by Scotch who dressed as described, and the influence they left impressed itself on the gentleman's sensitive brain.

"All houses where men have lived and died are haunted houses," not by actual ghosts, but by the subtile force which persons impart to everything with which they come in contact. That he was subject to some influence outside of himself is shown by the appearances always being of some one that he had never seen, and hence they could not have been revived pictures from his own brain. After he had been in the house for a long time he began to see his own face; that is, after he had imparted his own influence to his surroundings, he received them back as from a mirror.

Dendy, in his "Philosophy of Mystery," mentions "M. Andral, who in his youth saw, in La Pitie, the putrid body of a child covered with larvae, and during the next morning the spectre of this corpse lying on his table was as perfect as reality." He could not see it by a mental effort, nor any where else than on his table, and whenever he looked at that, the appearance at once came. It may be said in explanation, that the sight of the disgusting object produced a strong impression on the optic nerves and mind, and a suggestive object, as the table reproduced the same state. We have no evidence that one object, under the same light, affects the optic nerves more than any other would under the same circumstances. Vivid mental impressions are more readily reproduced than those that scarcely ruffle the surface of thought; but this does not account for the student not seeing the appearance at any other time or place than on the table where it had laid, and which we would say retained the influence imparted to it by the body having lain there.

Professor Hitchcock says that during a severe sickness, "day after day visions of strange landscapes spread out before him--mountain, lake and forest; vast rocks, strata upon strata piled to the clouds; the panorama of a world shattered and upheaved, disclosing the grim secrets of creation, the unshapely and monstrous rudiments of organic being." His son, Professor Charles Hitchcock, adds that his father saw the sandstone beds of the Connecticut valley spread out before him, covered with tracks, and by the superior insight wrought by sickness, cleared up some doubtful points to which he had vainly given his attention. Professor Hitchcock became, in consequence of his sickness, exceedingly sensitive, and the geological specimens near him, or that he had handled, brought up in his mind the pictures of their primeval age.

HALLUCINATIONS.--The received definition of an hallucination is a false perception without any material basis, being formed entirely in the mind. An individual who sees pictures on a blank wall, or who hears voices when no sound reaches his ear, is hallucinated. "The reason for this being that the erroneous perception constituting the hallucination is found in that part of the brain which ordinarily requires the excitation of sensorial impressions for its functions." In this view, hallucination is evidence of mental derangement and incipient insanity. This explanation is by no means sufficient for this class of facts. That a certain tract of brain can of itself give the mind complicated representations, never before seen or imaged in the mind, is not established. The reappearance of objects that have been seen is better explained, and still more satisfactorily, by causes which unite them all together, and with all like phenomena. George Combe says of a painter who inherited much of the patronage of Sir Joshua Reynolds, and believed himself to possess a talent superior to his, was so fully engaged that he had painted three hundred large and small portraits in one year. The fact appeared physically impossible, but the secret of his rapidity and astonishing success was this: He required but one sitting of his model. His method was as follows, as given by himself: "When a sitter came, I looked attentively on him for half an hour, sketching from time to time on the canvas. I did not require a longer sitting. I removed the canvas, and passed to another person. When I wished to continue the first portrait, I recalled the man to my mind. I placed him on the chair, where I perceived him as distinctly as though really there, and, I may add, in form and color more decidedly brilliant. I looked from time to time at the imaginary figure and went on painting, occasionally stopping to examine the picture exactly as though the original was before me; whenever I looked towards the chair I saw the man. This method made me very popular, and as I always caught the resemblance, the sitters were delighted that I spared them the annoying sittings of other painters."

This painter was far from incipient insanity. He was sensitive to impressions, and able by that organization to recall the image of the sitter, but not that of one who had not occupied the chair.

The Rev. T. L. Williams, Vicar of Porthleven, in The Journal of the Society for Psychical Research, July, 1885, gives his personal experience: "On an occasion when I was absent from home, my wife awoke one morning, and to her surprise and alarm saw me standing by the bedside looking at her. In her fright she covered her face with the bed clothes, and when she ventured to look again the appearance was gone. On another occasion, when I was not absent from home, my wife saw me, as she supposed, coming from church in surplice and stole. I came a little way, she says, and turned round the corner of the building, where she lost sight of me. I was at the time in the church in my place in the choir, where she was much surprised to see me on entering the building.... My daughter has often told me, and now repeats the story, that she was passing my study door, which was ajar, and looked in to see if I was there. She saw me in my chair, and as she caught sight of me, I stretched out my arms, and drew my hands across my eyes, a familiar gesture of mine. I was in the village at the time. Now, nothing occurred at or about the times of these appearances to give any meaning to them." He adds: "A good many years ago there was a devout young woman living in my parish, who used to spend much of her spare time in church in meditation and prayer. She used to assert that she frequently saw me standing at the altar when I certainly was not there in the body." Mr. Williams must have been a man peculiarly endowed with psychic force to thus impress himself.

The following is from the pen of the gifted Mary Howitt, and not only gives a remarkable fact, but her explanation of the same: "I conducted Mrs. Nenner through a room which contained some ancient furniture and a quantity of valuable old china. This china had been left in our care by a friend during his lengthened absence abroad. His thoughts from his place of sojourn at the antipodes constantly reverted to these heirlooms.

"'Who are these six gentlemen, evidently brothers, sitting where the old china is?' asked Mrs. Nenner, when we had passed through the room.

"'There was no one there at all,' I said, much surprised.

"'Then,' said she, 'I must have seen six brother spirits. There they were sitting; tall, fair men, light haired, all strikingly alike, all the same age. They must be brothers!'

"I recognized in her description the owner of the china. Before Mrs. Nenner left, we showed her a portrait of the owner of the china, our friend on the other side of the world. She at once said, 'Oh, that is one of the six brothers!' In some mysterious manner the intensity of thought fixed by the possessor of the china upon his possessions--we knew that his thoughts constantly reverted to them--had been able to manifest itself to the sight in the form of the man himself, but multiplied into six forms. It should be observed that this gentleman was of what now we should term a 'mediumistic' temperament. It is possible, that being at the antipodes, he might be, at the time his multiplied form was beheld, asleep--it being night there when it is day with us--and that his thoughts might have, in a dream, revisited England."

Since civilization began, mankind have held certain stones and metals as precious, and attributed rare qualities to charms, relics and amulets. We may indulge our mirth over the miraculous qualities ascribed to the bones of martyrs and the teeth of saints, a bit of wood from the true cross; but casting aside the rubbish gathered by imposture and credulity, we discover a great truth. Precious stones and metals have become so because of the subtile power of their emanations. In a true relic the sensitive perceives the full expression of the original owner's life, and feels it reproduced in him. As the phonograph treasures up the tone, the accent, the quality of the voice, and the thought of the speaker, so the relic preserves and constantly gives forth the character of the one it represents.

Shrines and holy places have cause for being regarded as sacred, and their preservation in purity for the one and only purpose is correct in science. The church devoted to the worship of Jehovah holds its devotees with the invisible bonds reaching out from the walls forged from the psycho-aura of all preceding worshippers. That the members hold their houses exclusively for certain uses may be the result of superstition, but they are right in thus doing. A church building given over during the week to shows and entertainments, and nightly filled with the class such would draw, would become so saturated with worldly influences as to be unfit for the promulgation of the highest religious thought on Sunday. Both audience and minister would feel the depressing effect, and religious zeal would reach zero.

How strong and enduring the impress stamped on a relic or jewel may be, is shown in the following story told of Robert Browning by Mr. Knowles (Spectator, Jan. 30, 1869): "Mr. Robert Browning tells me that when he was in Florence some years since, an Italian nobleman (Count Ginnasi) was brought to his house. The Count professed to have great mesmeric powers, and declared in reply to Mr. Browning's avowed skepticism, he would convince him of his powers. He then asked Mr. Browning whether he had anything about him then and there, which he could hand him, and which was in anyway a memento or relic. It so happened by curious accident, that Mr. Browning was wearing under his coat sleeves some gold wrist studs to his shirt, which he had quite recently taken into wear in absence of his ordinary wrist-buttons. He had never before worn them in Florence, or elsewhere, and found them in an old drawer where they had lain forgotten for years. One of these he took out and handed to the Count, who held it in his hand awhile and then said as if much impressed, 'There is something here which cries out in my ear, Murder! murder!'

"And truly," said Mr. Browning, "these studs were taken from the dead body of a great uncle of mine, who was violently killed on his estate in St. Kitts nearly eighty years ago. They were produced in court as proofs that robbery had not been the object of the strangler, which was effected by his own slaves. They were taken out of the night-gown in which he died and given to me."

Sensitiveness During Sleep.

The Index published the following:

"Recently the youngest child of Warren Wasson (Katie) fell into a well and was nearly drowned. A day or two since, a letter was received from Mr. Wasson, who is in Oregon, written before he had heard of the occurrence. He stated that on the same Sunday, at the time of the accident, he was taking a nap, and was awakened by a terrifying dream. He thought he saw little Katie dripping with water, and the little boy next older than Katie was immersed in the water, and that he was able to save him only by taking hold of his ears. When he pulled him out, he was covered with spots like a leopard. Mr. Wasson says that as he awoke he was covered with cold sweat, and in an agony of mind. This is a very strange coincidence, and the dream corresponds with the occurrence, save that the little boy was not in danger. It was the little girl who was spotted from the chill."

It resembles a wrongly received telegraphic dispatch, in which one word is substituted for another.

EFFECT OF STRONG MENTAL IMPRESSION.--A strong mental impression carried into sleep is conducive to impressibility. Inspector Jewett, of the Brooklyn Police, was so worried about the lost pistol of John Kenny, who had shot a car-driver, as he wanted the weapon in evidence against the ruffian, that he dreamed about it. He saw it in a certain saloon, in a certain place, and the next morning went to the saloon and found the pistol exactly where he saw it in his dream.

The rescue of the crew of the "Sparkenhoe," November 30, 1875, by Capt. Adam S. Smalley, as told by him, is a fine illustration of impressibility in sleep. He sailed from Bordeaux November 24, 1875, in the brigantine "Fred Eugene," bound for Key West, and soon encountered stormy weather. When six hundred miles at sea, on the night of the 29th, he suddenly awoke from sleep, deeply impressed with a dream, in which he had seen a number of men in great peril. He related this to his wife, adding that he hoped no shipwrecked crew needed his assistance. At midnight, he again retired, and again the vision was repeated with more distinctness, and the men appearing on a wreck needing the utmost dispatch to rescue them. The Captain went immediately on deck, and without any assigned reason, changed the course of the ship two points, and, giving orders to be called at daylight, retired, and slept till the appointed time.

Going on deck at dawn, and sweeping the horizon with his glass, he discovered a ship far to the windward, with a signal of distress displayed. He endeavored to work his vessel up, but with short sail and heavy sea, most of the forenoon passed, and a long distance remained. He was resolved to take a long tack, and not change his course until prompted to do so by the same impulse that bade him do so the night before. More sail was made, although prudence forbade, in the face of a gale at any moment threatening to break, and all the men stood at their posts for over an hour, awaiting the orders for tacking.

At last the prompting came, and going about, the vessel reached a point two miles to the leeward of the distressed ship, where her three boats, containing twenty-three men in all, had put off to intercept the brig. They were taken on board, the boats cut loose, and all sail taken in as quickly as possible, and in ten minutes a fierce hurricane lashed the sea to foam. The gale raged four days with unabated fury, so that, had they not been rescued at the very moment they were, they would have certainly perished.

We have two explanations. The first is that of thought transference--the reception on the sensitive brain of Captain Smalley of the intense thoughts of the perishing crew. As the inductive plate sends its influence across miles of space, we may suppose that the vibrations from them would go out across the wide sea interval, and, finding a receiving instrument, be converted again to thought. The second explanation is that of the interference of spiritual beings, who impress their thoughts on the mind of the Captain in the same manner. The prompting as to the course to steer is beyond and outside of the dream, and proves the extreme sensitiveness of the commander.

A DREAM SAVES A SHIPWRECKED CREW.--Of precisely similar character is the impression received by Capt. G. A. Johnson of the schooner "Augusta H. Johnson." He sailed from Quero for home, encountering a terrible hurricane. On the second day, he saw a disabled brig, and near by a barque. He was anxious to reach home, and thinking the barque would assist the brig, continued on.

But the impression came that he must turn back and board the brig. He could not shake it off, and at last he, with four men, boarded the brig in the dory. He found her deserted, and made sail on her. After a time they saw an object ahead, appearing like a man on a cake of ice. The dory was again manned, and sent to the rescue. It proved to be the mate of the bark "Leawood," clinging to the bottom of an overturned boat, which, being white, appeared in the distance as ice. This premonition came without seeking, and in direct opposition to the desire of Captain Johnson, desiring to escape from the storm, and reach home without delay.

A LIFE SAVED.--The Biddeford (Me.) Journal thus relates the story of the narrow escape of a sailor:

"Last week the schooner "Ida May" lay at Government Wharf, near the mouth of Kennebunk River, with one man on board, Freeman Grove, who was in the cabin asleep. In the night he was awakened by some one touching him and saying, 'You will be drowned.' On opening his eyes, no one was present, but he immediately went on deck, and found the side of the vessel caught under the wharf by the tide, and shortly it would have sunk, and cabin and all been under water. With a plank he pried the side from the wharf, and she came up with the tide. The sleeper, being in the cabin, must have been drowned had he not been awakened by the voice."

Perhaps no greater disaster was ever accompanied by a greater number of special premonitions and warnings of coming danger than the "Ashtabula horror," where a train crowded with passengers plunged into a gulf in a fearful storm, and, taking fire, was burned. The Times published a list of the names of those saved by "presentiments." One, in particular, is related at length, and is thoroughly vouched for. A young lady, by the name of Hazen, having with her a colored servant, started from Baltimore for Pittsburg, where she was to be married. She had purchased tickets at Buffalo for the ill-fated train. During the night previous, "Aunt Chloe," the colored slave, had a dream, which so impressed her that when they reached the depot she positively refused to go on that train. "Auntie" had been as a mother to Miss Hazen, who lost her mother in infancy. The young lady, perhaps somewhat a believer in the superstitions of the slaves, humored Auntie's mood, and deferred going until the next train--in all probability thereby saving the lives of both.

CLAIRVOYANT DREAM-STATE.--The Oakland (Cal.) Tribune records a pleasing story, which fully illustrates what may be called a permanent dream-sensitiveness identical with clairvoyance: "Twenty years ago, a bachelor in Oakland dreamed of visiting a family consisting of parents and two little girls, who were unknown to him in his waking hours. From that time forth, he continued to dream of them for a score of years. He saw the children grow from childhood to womanhood. He was at the closing exercises when they graduated. In fact, he shared all the pleasures and griefs of the family. His friendship to his dreamland friends seemed so real, he often remarked that he felt certain he would know them in reality at some future time.

"Two months ago, in a dream, he saw the husband die, and from that time he ceased to dream of them in a period of twenty years. He received a letter from New York City, the writer being the widow of a cousin of his, with whom he had had no intercourse since his boyhood--over thirty years. She wrote that she wished to make San Francisco her future home, and it was arranged for him to meet her and her two daughters at the wharf at Oakland. On their arrival, imagine his surprise to see his dream friends. They were equally so when he related to them the dreams in which they had figured. He told them incidents connected with their past lives which he could not have known under ordinary circumstances. He described their former home, even to the furniture and household ornaments, and was correct in every particular. The sequel is that he married the lady, and they are living happily in this city."

ALLEGORICAL DREAMS.--When important intelligence comes in allegorical form, it is difficult to give adequate explanation, without calling to our aid an outside intelligence. The London News has the following:

"Most people remember the terrible railway accident, in which Dickens himself and his proof-sheets escaped, while so many perished. In the train there chanced to be a gentleman and lady just returned from India. The lady said to her husband, 'I see the great wave rolling on; it is close to us,' and then the crash came, and she was a corpse. The husband was unhurt, and at a later time explained his wife's strange words. Ever since they had set sail from India, she had been haunted in sleep by a dream of a vast silvery wave, and always, just as it was about to break on her, she had awakened in terror."

Less tragic, but quite odd enough for Mr. Proctor's collection, is the anecdote of the south-country farmer's dream. The good man awakened from his first sleep, and aroused his wife to tell her about a startling vision. He had dreamed that he saw a favorite cow drowning in a pond in a neighboring common. "There ain't no pond there;" said the wife, with natural irritation and double-shotted negatives. This was undeniably true, but the farmer was uneasy. At last he arose, dressed, and walked up the long lane which led to the common. Everything was quiet, but just at the top of the lane the farmer heard a sound as of a man digging. Then a light caught his eye. It glimmered through a hedge that divided the lane from the fields. The farmer cautiously drew near, till he was just above the ditch. There he spied a country fellow, with a lantern, digging a long, straight, deep hole in the ground. An ax lay beside the hole. At this point the farmer slipped, the hedge rustled, and the delver fled away. The farmer secured the lantern and made for home. Just at the entrance of the lane, the time being about two in the morning, he met one of his servant wenches hurrying in the direction whence he had come. "What do you want, my lass? No good, I fear," said the agricultural moralist; and, in short, he made the girl tell him her story. She was going to an assignation with her "young man," who had jilted her, and was courting another girl. She had threatened him with an action for breach of promise of marriage, and the swain had promised that, if she would but meet him at two in the morning, at the bend of the lane, he would satisfy her, and remove all jealousy and differences.

"Very well, my lass," said the farmer, "come, and I'll show you what he had to give you." He led the way, and revealed to the horrified girl the long, deep, narrow hole and sharp ax which had awaited her. Naturally, she did not any longer pursue her lover; and here is a dream which even Mr. Proctor will admit not to have been purposeless. Indeed, the "machinery" of the drowning cow made the vision appeal directly to the bucolic mind.

Of the same prophetic character is the following well-authenticated dream:

Mrs. Jacob Condon, living a few miles from Reed, Pa., dreamed a few nights ago that her year-old baby was burned to death, and that she sent word of the casualty to her husband, who was working at a distance from home, by James Portlewaith, a neighbor. The next morning she told her husband of her dream, and admitted that it made her despondent. He laughed at her fears, and went away to his work. Late in the forenoon, Mrs. Condon left her kitchen to go to the wood-shed, a few steps away. While she was there she heard her baby screaming. She ran into the house and found the child lying in front of an open grate, wrapped in flames. She threw an old coat about the child, and smothered the flames, but it was so badly burned that it died in a few minutes. Mrs. Condon went to the door to call for assistance. As she reached the door, James Portlewaith was passing the gate. She sent him to her husband with the dreadful news, thus fulfilling her terrible dream to the letter.

Mrs. Howitt, whose veracity no one can dispute, gives the following experience in the Psychological Review, London, which may be taken as an illustration of thought transference, or as the interposition of a supreme intelligence:

"I dreamed that I received a letter from my eldest son. In my dream I eagerly broke open the seal, and saw a closely-written sheet of paper, but my eye caught only these words in the middle of the first page, written larger than the rest and underlined, 'My father is very ill.' The utmost distress seized me, and I suddenly awoke, to find it only a dream; yet the painful impression of reality was so vivid, that it was long before I could compose myself. The first thing I did the following morning was to commence a letter to my husband, relating this distressing dream. Six days afterwards, on the 18th, an Australian mail came in and brought me a letter, the only letter I received by that mail, and not from any of my own family, but from a gentleman in Australia with whom we were acquainted. This letter was addressed on the outside, 'Immediate,' and with a trembling hand I opened it; and true enough, the first words I saw--and these written larger than the rest, in the middle of the paper, and underlined, were: 'Mr. Howitt is very ill.' The context of these terrible words was, however, 'If you hear that Mr. Howitt is very ill, let this assure you that he is better;' but the only emphatic words which I saw in my dream, and these, nevertheless, slightly varying, as, from some cause or other, all such mental impressions, spirit revelations, or occult, dark sayings generally do vary from the truth or type which they seem to reflect."

Stainton Moses, M. D., who has given life-long attention to psychic research, remarks on the apparent discrepancy between the words of the dream, and the letter as follows:

"It may be permitted to the writer to suggest, that through a fuller acquaintance with, and deeper observation of, the phenomena of 'spirit revelation, occult, dark sayings', etc., the truth has forced itself upon various philosophic minds, that in obedience to a primal law of spirit's intercourse with spirit--it is always the essence or spirit of an idea or fact which is sought to be conveyed to the mind, and not the mere literal clothing of that idea or fact. This essence or spirit of the idea is the grain of true wheat alone needed; the form is simply the husk that clothes it for a temporary purpose, and must of necessity fall away from it as a dead thing. 'In this material, matter-of-fact age, literal truth,' says the Rev. James Smith, 'the lowest of all truths in one sense, is generally regarded as the highest. But they are superficial thinkers who dabble only in literal truth or physical truth.' This is a knowledge of Law Spiritual, without which progress is impossible for the student of psychology."

THE IDEA, NOT WORDS, CONVEYED.--If the idea was sent through the psychic-ether, as a wave of thought, it would translate itself into language, and the language of the receiving mind would be the one into which it would be translated. It would pass through space as the essence of thought, and the sensitive recipient would clothe it with the garments of words.

Wm. Howitt, on his visit to Australia, had a dream which he regarded as having great importance as a fact in Mental Science. He says:

"Some weeks ago, while yet at sea, I had a dream of being at my brother's at Melbourne, and found his house on a hill at the further end of the town, next to the open forest. The garden sloped a little way down the hill to some brick buildings below; and there were greenhouses on the right hand by the wall as you looked down the hill from the house. As I looked out the windows in my dream, I saw a wood of dusky-foliaged trees, having a segregated appearance in their heads; that is, their heads did not make that dense mass like our woods. 'There!' said I, addressing some one in my dream, 'I see your native forest of Eucalyptus!' This dream I told to my sons, and to two of our fellow-passengers, at the time, and on landing, as we walked over the meadows, long before we reached the town, I saw this very wood. 'There!' I exclaimed, 'is the very wood of my dream. We shall see my brother's house there.' And so we did. It stood exactly as I saw it, only looking newer; but there, over the wall of the garden, is the wood exactly as I saw it and now see it, as I sit at the dining-room window writing. When I look upon this scene I seem to look into my dream."

This mysterious perception of scenes and events which, after perhaps years, come before the dreamer or enter into his life, is supported by ample testimony.

In the Spiritual Magazine, 1871, the author, speaking of this dream, gives further curious details:

"In a vision at sea, some thousand miles from Melbourne, I not only clearly saw my brother's home and the landscape around it, but also saw things in direct opposition to news received before leaving England. It was said that all the men were gone to the gold-fields, and that even the Governor and Chief-Justice had no men-servants left. But I now saw abundance of men in the streets of Melbourne, and many sitting on doorsteps asking employment.... When in the street before my brother's house, we saw swarms of men, and some actually sitting on steps, seeking work. All was so exactly as I had described, that great was the astonishment of my companions."

If we were to regard sleep, after the common usage, as a simple state, dreams, visions, thought transference, and the appearance of a person while living at a distance, become a mass of irreconcilable details. But this is a wholly erroneous view of the character of sleep. It is one of the most complex and changeful conditions, ranging from the disturbed doze of the overweary, to the most sensitive clairvoyance. It will be seen that many of the so-called dreams are really visions received in a more sensitive condition than is furnished during the waking hours.

Dreams.

SENSITIVENESS DURING SLEEP.--There are dreams and dreams. When greatly fatigued, mentally or physically, the partially awakened faculties often become impressed with strangely distorted thoughts. Then there are the terrible dreams from indigestion, the peculiar interpretations of bodily discomfort, as dreams of frosts and snows, when chilled during sleep, or of burning forests when over-heated. Galen gives examples of such dreams in the case of a man who dreamed that his right leg was turned to stone, and soon after lost the use of it by palsy; and another patient who dreamed that he was in a vessel filled with blood, which the physician accepted as a sign that the man ought to be bled, by which a serious disease under which he labored was cured.

In perfect sleep dreams do not occur, because all the mental faculties are dormant. The conjecture that the mind always dreams, but fails to remember, is not true. A hearty supper, by inducing indigestion, is a prolific cause of bad dreams.

Derangement of the perfect correlation of the mental faculties, in sickness or the weakness of age, is a frequent cause of the wildest and most incoherent visions. All these causes may be well considered, and after their influences have been eliminated, there remains an order distinct and inexplicable by known causes. The dreamer may not be sensitive to psychic influences while awake, but during sleep may become exceedingly so. Night favors sensitiveness because of its negative influence. All nervous diseases are aggravated by the coming of twilight, and midnight is the hour when the most perfect negativeness is reached, as high noon is that of extreme positiveness.

It would be an easy task to fill volumes with dreams that have been received as premonitions of future events, or forecasts of desired information, which was otherwise impossible to obtain. I do not desire to crowd these pages with any more than will serve to illustrate the various characters of the true psychic dream, and show how the extra sensitiveness acquired in sleep explains this subject. It is misleading, however, to employ the word sleep in this connection, for in sound sleep there is dreamless rest. Sleep is the repose of the faculties, and impressions are not recognized. The peculiar condition in which these dreams occur, is mistaken for sleep, but is nearer trance. The silence of the night and its soothing negative quality, enhances this state, and impressions are borne into the receptive mind on the psycho-ether. Dreams that reach into the future and foretell events concealed from human ken, and which no reasoning or forethought can predict, are of interest as revealing glimpses of a new field of thought--that of prophecy.

In the "Glimpses of the Supernatural," is a dream related by a dignitary of the Church of England:

"My brother had left London for the country to preach for a certain society to which he was officially attached. He was in usual health, and I therefore had no cause to feel anxiety about him. One night my wife awoke me, finding that I was sobbing in my sleep, and asked me the cause. I said, "I have been to a small village, and I went up to the door of the inn. A stout woman came to the door. I said to her: 'Is my brother here?' She said, 'No, sir; he is gone.' 'Is his wife here?' I inquired. 'No, sir; but his widow is.'" Then the distressing thought came to me that my brother was dead. A few days after, I was suddenly summoned into the country. My brother had been attacked by a fatal illness, at Caxton. The following day his wife was summoned, and the next day, while they were seated together, she heard a sigh and he was gone. When I reached Caxton, it was the very village I had visited in my dream. I went to the same house, was let in by the same woman, and found my brother dead and his widow there."

The story told by Dean Stanley has been widely circulated. The chiefs of the Campbells, of Inverawe, gave an entertainment. After the party broke up, one of the guests returned, claiming protection, which Campbell pledged himself to give. It afterwards appeared, in a brawl, he had killed Donald, the cousin of Campbell, and notwithstanding his pledge, he ordered him away. The murderer appealed to the word of his host, and was allowed to stay for the night, where Campbell slept. The blood-stained Donald appeared to him saying: "Inverawe, Inverawe, blood has been shed; shield not the murderer." Having sent the guilty man away, the last time the vision came, saying: "Inverawe, Inverawe, blood has been shed. We shall not meet again until we meet at Ticonderoga."

In 1758, there was a war between France and England, and Campbell, belonging to the Forty-second Highlanders, went to America. On the eve of the engagement the general said to the officers, who knew of what they regarded as Campbell's superstition, that it was best not to tell him the name of the fortress they were to attack on the morrow, but call it Fort George. The fort was assaulted in the morning and Campbell mortally wounded. His last words were: "General, you have deceived me. I have seen him again. This is Ticonderoga."

Vouched for as this occurrence is by the highest authority, it is of great significance, not only as a dream, but it shows that death brought about a sensitive condition like that in which the dream was received, and enabled Donald to again appear.

Among the news items of the San Francisco Chronicle, appeared the following:

"Yesterday morning W. S. Read, of Oakland, with a companion named Stein, started out from Long Wharf to reach a yacht upon which they were going on a fishing excursion. When about two hundred yards from the wharf the boat was capsized and Read was drowned. He started to swim to the wharf, but when within fifty feet of it he sank and did not rise again. Connected with this sad event is a dream: Last Friday night the sister of the deceased dreamed that her brother had gone out in a boat on Sunday, that the boat had been upset and he drowned. So vivid was the impression of the dream, that on

Saturday morning she went to her brother's office, told him of it, and implored him not to go out, but he laughed at her fears as the result of a disordered mind."

Dr. M. L. Holbrook relates the following instances of dreams, which are certainly worth recording:

"Over twenty years ago I was subject to attacks of acute bronchitis, which in Spring gave me great trouble. On one occasion I was so exceedingly ill I felt I should not recover, and in this mood I fell to sleep, during which, in a dream, or what appeared to be such, my sister, who had died when I was a little boy, seemed to come to my bedside and said: 'Martin, you are not going to die; you have much important work yet to accomplish, and we have come to cure you.' Then what I can only describe as a shock of heavenly electricity struck me on the head, and was intensified over the lungs, where it seemed to almost burn through my chest, when it passed towards my feet in a delightful glow. The shock was so great that I awoke, free from the disease, and have never had the trouble since."

"In 1867 I was alone in my sleeping-room in New York, and dreamed that I was dying, and in my struggles awoke. There was nothing peculiar in this experience, it may be truthfully said, for this sensation is quite common with those who suffer with nightmare. The singularity of the case was that every night for a succession of nights the same thing happened, growing more and more intense, until the last night I thought I could not escape, and died. After it was over, the thought came to me, 'Well, it is not so bad after all; a rather pleasant experience!' At this moment my father-in-law, who had been dead several months, appeared to me. He was the same as when alive, but more spiritual and beautiful. He said: 'Martin, I have been endeavoring to show myself to you for several nights. Now I have succeeded, and shall trouble you no more.' That was the last of my disturbing dreams. My thoughts were not upon him. I have never been able to convince myself that the vision was not objective, though I know some may not look at it in the same light."

Dr. A. M. Blackburn, of Cresco, Iowa, a well-known physician of that town, dreamed that he was called to visit a little girl in the neighboring town of Ridgeway. On his return he came to a broad river which it was impossible to cross. While waiting on the banks, an old friend, long since dead, appeared and assisted him in crossing. When the doctor arose in the morning he related his dream, and so strongly was he impressed with its prophetic meaning that he secured a policy on his life, talked over and arranged his business, and having adjusted all his affairs, he awaited the fatality he said was sure to overtake him. A day or two after, he was called to Ridgeway to visit a little girl, and on his return his horse ran away and he was killed. There is an allegorical element in this dream, and the presence of a departed friend who assists him over the stream, gives it a poetic cast. Yet who can say that it was not realized?

A dream is related by J. Crysler, of Republic City, Kansas, which proved not only true, but the elements of "the double," or of the appearance of the dreamer in the place he dreamed about, is introduced. He said, while from home he dreamed that his wife was sick, and awoke. On falling asleep again, the dream was repeated, a thing that had never before occurred to him. He remarked to a friend in the morning, that if he believed in dreams he would go directly home, as he felt troubled. He, however, waited and completed his business, reaching home the next day, when he found his wife just recovering from a severe attack of illness. Their three-year-old boy lodged with his mother, and became restless. All at once he asked: "Ma, what man is that standing there?" "Why," she replied, "I see no one." "Oh!" said he, "it is pa!" and turning over, contentedly dropped to sleep. The thoughts of the father, intensified by his solicitude, struck the sensitive brain of his child with such a force as to produce the impression that the father was an objective reality.

A prophetic dream must be impressed on the receiving mind, from a source having more than human intelligence. There must be a mind back of the impressions, capable of comprehending cause and effect more clearly than mortals are able to do. The effect cannot rise above its cause.

Laugh at the fantasies of a fevered brain, or the visions produced by a gorged stomach; the nightmare of the gourmand; the ghost-seeing of the dyspeptic; but there remain the dreams of the clear head and pure heart as angel visitants, and these should be treasured. When we rest in the arms of sleep, she hushes us with hymns sung by angelic voices, and sweet visions of the morning land.

Sensitiveness Induced by Disease.

Disease, by weakening the physical powers, is often conducive to a wonderful sensitiveness. In some cases of fever, the senses are wrought to an astonishing acuteness, especially hearing, the patient being disturbed by even the ticking of a watch in a remote room. The inner perception at other times is made equally acute. If the pulsations of sound become so magnified and painful, the waves of thought in the psycho-ether may become equally magnified, and reproduce the thoughts which sent them forth to the mind of the recipient. Many of the facts given in illustration of other phases of sensitiveness apply equally well here.

"Mademoiselle N---- was convalescing after a very prolonged illness, which had reduced her to a state of extreme weakness. All her family had gone to church, when a violent storm arose. Mademoiselle N---- went to the window to watch its effects; the thought of her father suddenly struck her, and, under existing circumstances, she felt much uneasiness. Her imagination soon persuaded her that her father had perished. In order to conquer her fears she went into a room in which she was accustomed to see him in his arm-chair. On entering, she was very much surprised at seeing him in his place, and in his accustomed attitude. She immediately approached to inquire how he had come in, and in addressing him, attempted to place her hand on his shoulder, but encountered only space. Very much alarmed, she drew back, and turning her head as she left the room, still saw him in the same attitude. More than half an hour elapsed from the time she first saw the apparition. During this time Mademoiselle N----, who was convinced that it was an illusion, entered the room several times, and carefully examined the arrangement of the objects, and especially of the chair." (De Boismont, page 276.)

Nothing had occurred to her father, and the appearance may be adequately accounted for on psychometric grounds. The chair was vibrant with the influence of the father, and those vibrations constantly carried out with them his image.

Mrs. Denton, an extremely sensitive person, relates an experience which shows how exactly similar the impressibility which may be called normal in contradistinction to that induced by disease. On entering a car from which the passengers had gone to dinner, she was surprised to see the seats occupied.

"Many of them were sitting perfectly composed, as if, for them, very little interest was attached to this station, while others were already in motion (a kind of compressed motion), as if preparing to leave. I thought this somewhat strange, and was about turning to find a seat in another car, when a second glance around showed me that the passengers, who had appeared so indifferent were really losing their identity, and, in a moment, were invisible to me. I had had time to note the personal appearance of several; and taking a seat I awaited the return of the passengers, thinking it more than probable I might in them find the prototypes of the faces and forms I had a moment before so singularly beheld. Nor was I disappointed. A number of those who returned to the cars I recognized as being, in every particular, the counterparts of their late but transient representatives."

Mary Dana Shindler, in the Voice of Truth, says:

"An aunt of ours was very ill with fever, and her only brother, commanding a packet ship between Havana and Charleston, was daily expected; but we feared he would arrive too late to see his sister in earth-life. One morning while we were watching at her bedside, she suddenly sat up, clapped her hands, and exclaimed joyfully, 'Brother William has come!' We all thought her mind wandering; but in about ten minutes he arrived at her house, and from that moment she began to recover. She could not tell us how she discovered that he had arrived, but only said, 'I knew it; I heard, and felt him.'"

Bishop Bowman, in a sermon delivered in Philadelphia, narrated a remarkable experience, which shows how near the state of death approaches trance or clairvoyance. The usual light treatment of the fact of the result of cerebral disturbance is far from a satisfactory solution:

"On my return from Japan, I preached in California, and probably overworked myself. The last Sunday in February, after holding divine service in my St. Louis Church, I returned home, when I was immediately taken sick with a lingering fever, which the physicians predicted would end fatally. At this point I seemed to fall into a kind of ecstasy, and I did not know whether I was alive or dead. I imagined I was on board a magnificent ship, and heard the captain say, 'Stop her,' which I thought to be the voice of my Divine Master, when my young eighteen-months-old child, who had died twenty years ago, came to me and said that she had heard that I was coming, and had come to meet me. After some conversation which I do not recollect, she said, 'Do you think I have grown, papa?' She then arose in a form of glory I have never before witnessed, and never again expect to see until I die, and then returned to her usual state, saying that she came in that shape to see if I would know her. She said that many other friends had inquired after me, and that an old gentleman and lady had taken her up and kissed her, saying that her papa was their boy. I then asked her where her mama was. 'Oh, she is away doing something for the Lord, but will meet us on our arrival at the wharf.' It was a season of great preciousness to me. It seems to me that I have come back from the other world; and although it is peculiar for me to say I was dead, it seems to me I was not in the body."

The testimony of those who have approached nearest to death, and have been brought back to life, favors, if not proves, that at that great crisis, as the senses fail, spiritual sensitiveness becomes acute, and the perceptions merge into a universal consciousness. A gentleman while swimming failed to sustain himself, and before assistance could reach him, sank, as he supposed, to rise no more.

"Then he saw, as if in a wide field, the acts of his own being, from the first dawn of memory until the time he entered the water. They were all grouped and ranged in the order of the succession of their happening, and he read the whole volume of existence at a glance; nay, its incidents and entities were photographed on his mind, illumined by light, the panorama of the battle of life lay before him." ("Sleep, Memory and Sensation," page 43.)

Clairvoyance has, as thus appears, a retrospection, and is as able to see the past as the present, or previse the future. The element of time does not appear to enter into the cognition of events by this faculty. Everything is in the present, and the past is only distinguished by order of sequence.

A gentleman in Iowa related to me his experience while insensible from the effect of cold. He was overtaken by a fearful storm, such as sometimes sweep across the prairies, and, losing his way after hours of vain struggling, sank exhausted in a drift of snow. The past events of his life came in a panoramic show before him, but so rapidly moving, that from boyhood until that moment was as an instant; then came a sense of perfect physical happiness, and he began dimly to see the forms of those whom he had known while living, but were now dead. They grew more and more distinct, but just as they came near and were, as he thought, overjoyed to receive him, darkness came suddenly and great pain; the vision faded, and he became conscious of the presence of his friends who had rescued him, and were applying every measure to restore him to life. How near he had reached the boundary line, the "dead line" beyond, from which there is no return to the body, was shown by his crippled hands and feet.

It is a singular fact that no one has ever recovered from a near approach to this line, who does not tell the same tale of an exalted perception and intensification of the mental faculties. Sometimes this is exhibited by the recognition of an event then transpiring, with which the subject is intimately connected, as in the following, wherein the deaths of near relatives or friends are discerned:

It is a historical fact that Rev. Joseph Buckminster, who died in Vermont, in 1812, just before his death, announced that his distinguished son, Rev. J. S. Buckminster, was dead.

The Eaton (O.) Telegraph gives the following parallel case: "On Wednesday morning last, at four o'clock, Gen. John Quince breathed his last. But a few minutes after that, Joseph Deem, who also died on the 14th, aroused from his sleep, and said to his son John, who attended him, 'Gen. Quince is dead.' To this John replied, 'You are mistaken, father, Gen. Quince is well, and goes by after his mail every day.' 'Yes,' said Father Deem, 'Gen. Quince is dead.' Shortly after a neighbor came in, and said that Gen. Quince had suddenly died."

Whenever the power of expression is retained, we see the development of clairvoyance at the approach of death. Sometimes the paralysis of the muscles prevents vocal expression, but where this is the case, the eyes show the ecstasy which the lifting of the vail from a new world only can give.

Mrs. Helen Willmans relates this touching story of the death of her child:

"From her birth she had been afraid of death. Every fiber of her body and soul recoiled from the thought of it.

"'Don't let me die!' she said. 'Don't let me die! Hold me fast--I can't go.'

"'Jenny,' I said, 'you have two little brothers in the other world, and there are thousands of tender-hearted people over there, who will love and take care of you.'

"But she cried despairingly, 'Don't let me go. They are strangers over there.'

"But even as she was pleading her little hands relaxed their clinging hold from my waist, and lifted themselves eagerly aloft; lifted themselves with such a straining effort that they raised the wasted body from its reclining position among the pillows. Her eyes filled with the light of divine recognition. They saw plainly something we could not see. But even at that supreme moment she did not forget to leave a word of comfort for those who gladly would have died in her place. 'Mamma! mamma! they are not strangers. I am not afraid!' And every instant the light burned more gloriously in her blue eyes, until at last it seemed as her soul leaped forth upon its radiant waves, and in that moment her trembling form relapsed among the pillows, and she was gone."

Thus we perceive that sensitiveness, which is first manifested in the mesmeric state, breaks in at rare intervals, during wakefulness or sleep, as vivid impressions or dreams, arises to clairvoyance as the spirit and physical body are separated more and more, and reaches its most intense expression at the moment of death, when the union between the two is severed.

It is after this great event that the spiritual being, formed from attenuated substance, far beyond the horizon of the most ethereal known to the senses, is free from the environments of the physical body. It sees, hears, feels, with the organization of its new being, and is cognizant of a world unknown to the mortal senses.

Thought Transference.

The English Society for Psychical Research have given greater attention to thought transference than any other subject which has engaged its attention, claiming that if it be proved, it becomes the foundation for a working theory, co-ordinating a vast number of related facts and phenomena. It was the conclusion of the committee after numerous experiments, that thought reading was an established fact. The adage, "The devil is near when you talk about him," is proven daily; for when an individual is going to a certain place expecting to meet certain ones, his thoughts go before him, and impress themselves. When those connected by intimate relations think of each other, their thoughts vibrate in responsive brains. Distance has inappreciable influence on the transference of thought. It may take place in the same room, or when the two persons are thousands of miles apart. As a personal experience I will relate one of many similar incidents which have awakened my attention to this wonderful phenomenon. Sitting by my desk one evening, suddenly as a flash of light, the thought came to write an article for the Harbinger of Light, published at Melbourne, Australia. I had by correspondence become acquainted with the editor, W. H. Terry, but there had been no letters passed for nearly a year. I had not thought of him or his journal, for I do not know how long a time, and I was amused at first with the idea of writing on the subject suggested. But the impression was so strong that I prepared and forwarded an article. Nearly two months passed before I received a letter from Mr. Terry requesting me to write an article on the subject, on which I had written, and making due allowance for time, the dates of our letters were the same. In our experience this crossing of letters answering each other, has twice occurred, the second by Mr. Terry answering a request of mine.

I have gathered a series of facts illustrative and demonstrative, by their culminative evidence. If any one statement be questioned as improbable, we must consider the probabilities increase with each and every instance corroboratory, and when a constantly augmenting series continue in the same line, each number adding strength to the others, the probability becomes a certainty.

Dr. Nicolas, Count de Gonemys, of Corfu, gives his personal experience in March number, 1885, of the Journal of the Society for Psychical Research:

"In the year 1869 I was officer of health in the Hellenic army. By command of the War Office I was attached to the garrison of the Island of Zante. As I was approaching the Island in a steamboat, to take up my new position, and about two hours distance from the shore, I heard a sudden inward voice say to me over and over in Italian, 'Go to Voterra.' I had no association with the name of M. Voterra, a gentleman of Zante, with whom I was not even acquainted, although I had once seen him, ten years before. I tried the effect of stopping my ears, and of trying to distract myself by conversation with the bystanders, but all was useless, and I continued to hear the voice in the same way. At last we reached the land; I proceeded to my hotel and busied myself with my trunks, but the voice continued to harass me. After a time a servant came and announced to me that a gentleman was at the door who wished to speak to me at once. 'Who is the gentleman?' I asked. 'M. Voterra,' was the reply. M. Voterra entered, weeping violently, in uncontrollable distress, imploring me to follow him at once, and see his son who was in a dangerous condition. I found a young man in maniacal frenzy, naked in an empty room, and despaired of by all the doctors of Zante for the past five years."

By magnetism Dr. Nicolas effected a perfect cure, the maniac becoming in the mesmeric state clairvoyant.

The following is by C. Ede, M. D., Guilford (J. S. P. R., July, 1882).

"Lady G. and her sister had been spending the evening with their mother, who was in her usual health and spirits when they left her. In the middle of the night the sister awoke in a fright, and said to her husband, 'I must go to my mother at once; do order the carriage. I am sure she is ill.' The husband, after trying in vain to convince his wife that it was only a fancy, ordered the carriage. As she was approaching the house where two roads met, she saw Lady G.'s carriage. When they met each asked the other why she was there. The same reply was made by both. 'I could not sleep, feeling sure my mother was ill, and so I came to see.' As they came in sight they saw their mother's confidential maid at the door, who told them when they arrived, that their mother had been taken suddenly ill, and was dying, and had expressed an earnest wish to see her daughters."

The daughters having so recently parted from their mother, made them peculiarly susceptible to her influence.

T. W. Smith, Ealing, W. England (J. S. P. R., July, 1882), had this experience, showing the close bonds which unite husband and wife:

"I left my house, ten miles from London, in the morning as usual, and in the course of the day was on the way to Victoria Street, when, in attempting to cross the road made slippery by the water cart, I fell, and was nearly run over by a carriage coming in an opposite direction. The fall and the fright shook me considerably, but beyond that I was uninjured. On reaching home, I found my wife waiting anxiously, and this is what she related to me: She was in the kitchen when she suddenly dropped, exclaiming, 'My God, he's hurt!' Mrs. S. who was near her heard the cry, and both agreed as to the time, etc."

The Rev. P. H. Newham (J. S. P. R., Feb. 1887), relates an extended series of experiments in will power. He was able while in church to draw the attention of any one in the audience by simply directing his thoughts to them. He experimented at a series of concerts, selecting those in front of him so that they could not catch his eye by simply raising their heads. "It was very interesting," he writes, "to see them first fidget about in their seats and at last turn their heads around and look about them, as if to see whence the uncomfortable feeling that influenced them proceeded."

The London Spectator for Christmas, 1881, contains an interesting story by A. J. Duffield, of thought transference. The gist of this story is that a Mr. Strong went to Lake Superior and became foreman of the Franklin copper mine. He fell sick and would have died but for the care of a lady whose husband was a director of the mining company. She had him carried to her own house, and nursed him with kindest care until he recovered. Seven years after this event, when he had drifted away from the mines, he was sitting by himself one evening, when he suddenly saw this kind lady in a room with nothing in it, no fire, no food. She was calm and quiet, with the same face she had when she nursed him in the fever. He thereby was made deeply conscious that she was in distress, and sent her a most liberal amount of money by mail. The day after he received a letter from the lady, saying that her husband was sick, and that they were in great suffering, and asking for aid.

In this instance the mind of Capt. Strong was bound to his preserver with strong bonds, love, gratefulness and expectation of some time repaying his great obligation. It was in proper condition for the reception of such thoughts, while, on the other hand, under the pressure of suffering, the lady's mind was in a condition to give force to the emanating thoughts.

The Springfield Homestead published what it called an odd circumstance, but so far from being odd is of proverbially common occurrence. A Mrs. A. and her daughter called on their relative, Mrs. B., of Central Street. On their way thither they remarked how pleased they would be if Mrs. B.'s daughter, Mrs. L., of Hartford, could only be there too. This remark was repeated to Mrs. B., and she replied that her thoughts were similar. Then one of them recalled the old saying that the combined thoughts of three women can bring any one from any place, and the reply was made that if wishing would bring Mrs. L. she would surely come. Mrs. B. prepared strawberry cake, saying her daughter, Mrs. L., was fond of it, and that she was going to lay a plate for her just as though she were there. As they were sitting down to tea, the door bell rang and in came the much wished for Mrs. L., greatly to their surprise. When asked how she happened to come, she replied that she did not intend to do so until that day, and decided to do so because tormented with the impression that some one wanted to see her. She is not accustomed to come to Springfield, not having visited her sister before in a year.

Henry Watson, of Mill Village, Pa., was suddenly impressed that his services were needed at a certain point on French Creek. There was no assignable cause for his going, and he resisted it as a vagary. The impression, however, grew so strong that he yielded as to a charm. When within a short distance of the spot cries for help reached his ears. In the creek he found George Dowler and wife struggling for their lives. They had attempted to ford the creek, and missing the way were submerged. He was holding on to the horse while the swift current was carrying his wife to her death. Taking a boat, Watson rescued her from certain death. Had he not arrived at that very moment, she would have been inevitably drowned.

L. M. Hastings of Osceola, Iowa, had a son murdered near Grand Island, Neb. The night after the crime was committed he awoke about midnight with his attention fixed on an apparition at the foot of the bed. He saw the representation of two men with great distinctness, and something told him that they were the pictures of the murderers of his son. He studied them carefully until they faded out of sight, and then arose and wrote a description which was forwarded to the prosecuting attorney. It was found to be a thoroughly accurate description of the men who were then under arrest and who were, without doubt the guilty parties. Mr. Hastings had never seen these men nor received any description of them.

TRANSFERENCE OF THOUGHT AND PAIN.--Mrs. Arthur Severn, the distinguished landscape painter (J. S. P. R., March, 1884), writes of an accident to her husband which at once impressed itself on her:

"I woke with a start, feeling I had a hard blow on my mouth, and a distinct sense that I had been cut under my upper lip, and held my handkerchief to the part as I sat up in bed, and after a few seconds, when I removed it, I was astonished not to see any blood, and only then realized that it was impossible that anything could have struck me, and so I thought it was only a dream. I looked at my watch and saw it was seven, and finding Arthur (my husband) was not in the room, I concluded he had gone out on the lake for a sail as it was fine.

"At breakfast (half-past nine) Arthur came in rather late, and I noticed he rather purposely sat farther away from me than usual, and put his handkerchief to his lip in the way I had done. I said: 'Arthur, why are you doing that? I know you have hurt yourself; but I'll tell you why afterwards.' He said: 'Well, when I was sailing, a sudden squall came, throwing the tiller suddenly around, and it struck me a hard blow in the mouth under the upper lip and it has been bleeding a good deal and won't stop.' I then asked: 'At what time did it happen?' He answered: 'It must have been about seven o'clock.' I then told what had happened to me, much to his surprise and all who were at the table."

Rev. J. M. Wilson, head master of Clifton College (in J. S. P. R., March, 1884), presents a fact which, while admitting of telegraphic explanation, may be referred to a higher source:

"I was at Cambridge at the end of my second term in full health, boating, football playing, and the like, and by no means subject to hallucinations or morbid fancies. One evening I felt very ill, trembling with no apparent cause; nor did it seem to me at the time to be a physical illness, or chill of any kind. I was frightened; I was totally unable to overcome it. I remember a struggle with myself, resolving that I would go on with my mathematics, but it was in vain. I became convinced that I was dying. I went down to the room of a friend, who was on the same staircase. He exclaimed at me before I spoke. He pulled out a whisky bottle and backgammon board, but I could not face it. We sat over the fire, and he brought some one else to look at me. Toward eleven, after some three hours, I got better, went to bed and after a time to sleep, and next morning was quite well. In the afternoon came a letter stating that my twin brother had died the evening before in Lincolnshire."

Rev. Canon Warburton, Winchester, England (J. S. P. R., May 1884), relates the following, which is of interest as an example of transference of thought and of sensation:

"I went from Oxford to stay a day or two with my brother, then a barrister at 10 Fish Street, Lincoln's Inn. When I reached his chambers I found a note on the table apologizing for his absence, and saying he had gone to a dance, and intended to be at home soon after one o'clock. Instead of going to bed, I dozed in an arm-chair, but started up wide awake exactly at one, ejaculating, 'By Jove, he's down!' and seeing him coming out of the drawing room into the brightly illuminated landing, catching his foot in the edge of the top stair and falling head-long, just saving himself by his elbows and hands. (The house was one I had never seen, and I did not know where he was.) I again fell adoze for half an hour, and was awakened by my brother suddenly coming in and saying: 'Ah! there you are! I have just had as narrow an escape of breaking my neck as I ever had in my life. Coming out of the ballroom, I caught my foot and tumbled full length down stairs.'"

The following is vouched for by Miss Millicent Ann Page, sister of the Rev. A. Shaw Page, Vicar of Lesly, England, to whom it was related by Mrs. Elizabeth Broughton, Edinburgh:

"Mrs. Broughton aroused her husband, telling him something dreadful had happened in France. He begged her to go asleep again. She assured him that she was not asleep when she saw what she insisted in then telling him. First, a carriage accident, which she did not see, but she saw the result: a broken carriage, collected crowd, a figure gently raised and carried into the nearest house, and then a figure lying on the bed, which she recognized as the Duke of Orleans. Gradually friends collected around the bed, among them several members of the royal family--the Queen, then the King--all tearfully, silently watching the dying Duke. One man, she could see his back, but did not know who he was, was a doctor. He stood bending over the Duke, feeling his pulse with his watch in his other hand. Then all passed away. In the morning she wrote down in her journal all she had seen. It was before the days of the telegraph, and two or more days passed before the Times announced the death of the Duke of Orleans.

"A short time after, she visited Paris, recognized the place of the accident, and received an explanation of her impression. The doctor who attended the Duke was an old friend of hers; and as he watched by the bed he said his mind was constantly occupied with her and her family. The reason, therefor, was the remarkable likeness between the members of her family and those of the royal family then present. 'I spoke of you and yours when I reached home, and thought of you many times that evening,' said the doctor. 'The likeness between yourself and the royal family was never so strong. Here was a link between us, you see.'"

Certain dreams may be explained by thought-transference, which is liable to take place during the varying moods of slumber as while awake. Rev. J. C. Learned writes (J. S. P. R.): "It was in 1883 that I took charge of the Unitarian Church in Exeter, N. H. Five miles away, Rev. A. M. Bridge was preaching at Hampton Falls, with whom I sometimes exchanged pulpits. After a year or so he gave up the work in this little parish, and somewhat later entered upon an engagement in the town of East Marshfield, Mass., as the railroad runs, eighty miles from Exeter.

"On Wednesday, Dec. 13th, 1865, on waking in the morning, I remarked to my wife upon the very vivid and singular dream which I had had, and related it fully. I had seen Mr. Bridge taken suddenly and violently ill. He seemed to be in a school-room. He sank down helpless and was borne away by friendly hands. I was by him, and assisted others in whatever way I could. But he grew worse; the open air did not revive him; a leaden pallor soon spread over his features; peculiar spots which I had never seen before, like moles or discoloration of the skin, appeared upon his face, and after much suffering he died. Immediately after breakfast, and while we were still speaking of the dream, a ring at the door admitted Mr. Wells Healy, an old parishioner of Mr. Bridge, at Hampton Falls. I guessed the nature of his message. He had come to ask me to attend the funeral services of his former minister.

"I attended the funeral as requested. I learned from the family the particulars of his death, which coincided remarkably in several points with the dream already repeated to my wife, and when I looked at the dead man in his coffin, my attention was fixed by the peculiar spots on his face to which I have alluded, and which were stamped on my memory."

DOUBLE PRESENCE.--APPEARANCE OF LIVING PERSONS AT A DISTANCE.--It would appear that this projection of thought to distant localities may be so strong as to carry the appearance of the projector with it. This may be explained by the aid of psychometry, or by the actual projection of the psychic individuality, so as to give the impression of identity, and not only that, but to receive and retain impressions on the part of the projector. The double presence which has so perplexed the student of these mysteries thus admits of solution, and becomes a part of the fabric created by sensitiveness to thought impressions. These appearances of living persons as apparitions or ghosts, have been repeatedly employed as evidence of the subjectiveness of ghostly apparitions of the dead; that as one must be unreal so must the other. But this conclusion is unwarranted, as by the principles here advocated the apparitions of the living are under the same law as those of the dead.

It is possible for the independent clairvoyant at any time, in spirit, to visit distant localities and persons, and if the latter are sufficiently sensitive, they will recognize the clairvoyant's presence. The phenomenon of "double presence," in this manner can be produced, as somnambulism may be, by artificial means; that is through mesmerism or hypnotism.

Many remarkable stories are recorded of the double, some of which are unbelievable unless the principles heretofore stated are understood.

Josiah Gilbert, in the London Speculator, gives the following pleasing narrative:

"A son of a family named Watkinson, residing in Lancashire, had gone to America. One summer Sunday afternoon, they were attending services and occupying a large square pew near the pulpit. It was hot, the door of the small building was wide open, and one of the party who sat looking down the aisle could see out into the meeting-house yard, which was shaded by tall trees. Suddenly, to his intense surprise, he saw the absent brother approaching through the trees, enter at the chapel door, walk up the aisle, come to the very door of the pew itself, and lay his hand upon it as though he would take a seat with them. At that moment others of the family saw him also, but at that instant he vanished.

"This strange occurrence naturally raised sad forebodings, but in course of time a letter arrived, and it appeared that the brother was alive and well. He was then written to and asked if anything peculiar had happened on that Sunday. He replied that it was odd that he should remember anything about a Sunday so long passed, but certainly something had happened on that Sunday. He had come in overpowered with heat and had thrown himself on his bed, fallen asleep and had a strange dream. He found himself among the trees of a country chapel; service was going on; he saw them all, the door being open, sitting in their pews; he walked up the aisle and put his hand on the pew door to open it, when he suddenly, and to his great chagrin, awoke."

S. F. Deane, M. D., of Carlton, Neb., had a remarkable experience which he relates as follows:

"After my arrival in Nebraska, I made my home with my daughters. At the time I left Wisconsin, my wife was not well and I hesitated to leave her. After I had been absent about three weeks, I had retired to my room, which had a door opening into the street. About two o'clock in the morning while awake, with sufficient light from a partially obscured moon to see distinctly any person in the room, fully conscious of all my surroundings, and with my face toward the door, I saw it open and a person step into the room, which I at once recognized as the exact image of my wife. She came directly across the room, knelt at my bedside, put her arms about my neck, kissed me and said she had been very sick but was better now. Then she said she must go and see Adelaide, and arose and passed across the room, to the door of our daughter's room. She was gone a few minutes when she again came through the open bedroom door into my room, looked at me, as much as to say good-bye, passed out at the door, and was gone.

"While she was present a peculiar calmness came over me; but when she was gone a great anxiety took possession of me, and could I have taken a train, I should have at once started for home. But I at last resolved to await a letter, which came in due time from my son. He wrote: 'Mother is quite sick, though better than night before last, when about half-past two or three o'clock in the morning we thought for twenty or thirty minutes she was dead. She lay insensible, pulsation ceased, or only fluttered at intervals, and respiration seemed suspended, but she rallied and is now in a fair way to recover.' She did recover and enjoyed a fair degree of health."

There is no limit to the facts of this class which might be collected. Enough have been here produced to show that coincidence offers a poor apology as an explanation. The student will observe also, that however carefully the facts are selected bearing on this one point of thought transference, it is impossible, so intimately related are the branches of psychic science, to have them entirely free from the possibility of other explanations. Granting that thought may be transferred from one mortal to another, admits that a spirit may transfer its thoughts to a mortal also, and hence a spirit seeing a friend in distress may act as a messenger. But in such a case thought is transferred, and in the same manner. The sensitive on one side receives the pulsations of thought from the other, through and by means of the psychic ether.

It will be thus seen that there is no mystery in one mind becoming cognizant of the thoughts of another mind, for if in sympathy, such a result is sure to follow. As a lamp gives light, because it is able to set the light medium in motion, or give off waves therein, so the brain gives off waves, or is a pulsating center in the psychic-ether. These waves go outward and form the sphere of the individual, as the waves of light go out and form the sphere of light around an incandescent body.

To be recognized, they must strike against a sensitive or sympathetic brain, wherein they may be reproduced. By sympathetic, we mean one which, for want of a better term, we will say is similarly attuned. Thus, when two musical instruments are placed at some distance from each other, and one is played, if they are not attuned in harmony the other will give no response; but if they are, then when one is touched, the other answers note for note.

The brain, being a pulsating center, its thoughts, as they go out in waves, have to other brains, a tangible representation. The psychic-ether, pulsating with innumerable waves, may be regarded as a universal thought atmosphere, and the sensitive brain is able to gather from it thoughts and ideas which its pulsations express.

If any reliance can be placed on the observations of the most credible witnesses, whose evidence would be received on any other subject, and in law would be given power to decide on life or death, these facts of Thought Transference cannot be rejected. If they are received, they demand explanation. If thought passes from one mind to another, or, as it is often expressed, the will influences a distant person, it is self-evident that something passes from one to the other. What is this something? Facts conflict with the hypothesis of its being matter radiated from one individual to another, as light was once supposed to be transmitted. It passes too readily through vast thicknesses of solid matter, and is too instantaneous in its action, to consist of radiant particles. On the other hand, all of its phenomena show a striking relationship to light, heat and kindred forces.

HOW IS THIS INFLUENCE EXERTED?--Admitting that there is a psychic-ether, in which thinking produces waves, how does one individual influence another thereby? If the brain vibrates like the strings of a musical instrument, as no two are alike, no two vibrate alike. This is more than a mere illustration. Both depend on similar laws, for the string excites vibrations in the air, which are felt by the nerves of the tympanum of the ear. Thinking creates undulations in ether, which are impressed on other minds. The string of the instrument excites similar vibrations in contiguous strings; for the atmosphere transmits the waves of sound.

This is very beautifully shown by a simple experiment, which equally well illustrates the method by which mind influences mind. If a plate of glass is strewn with sand, and, while held in a horizontal position, a bow drawn across its edge, a musical sound will be produced from the vibration of the plate, and the sand, by the impulse, forms into various geometric lines, according to the note produced--each note giving rise to a figure peculiar to itself. So invariably is this the case that a piece of music might be accurately written from the forms assumed by the sand.

Now, if a piece of parchment or paper be stretched, with proper precautions, across the top of a large bell glass and strewn with sand, and the glass plate held over it horizontally, and the bow drawn across its edge, the forms assumed by the sand on the paper will accurately correspond with the forms on the glass. If the glass is slowly removed to greater and greater distances, the correspondence will continue until the distance becomes too great for the air to transmit the vibrations.

When a slow air is played on a flute near this apparatus, each note calls up a particular form in the sand, which the next note effaces and establishes its own. The motion of the sand will even detect sounds that are inaudible.

Professor Wheaton devised a means of beautifully illustrating this sympathy. If a sounding board is placed so as to resound to all the instruments of the orchestra, and connected by a metallic rod of considerable length with the sounding-board of a harp or piano, the instrument will accurately repeat the notes transmitted.

The nervous system, in its two-fold relation to the physical and spiritual being, is inconceivably more finely organized than the most perfect musical instrument, and is possessed of finer sensitiveness.

But it must not be inferred that all minds are receptive. Light falls on all substances alike, but is very differently affected. One class of bodies absorbs all but the yellow rays; another, all but the blue; another, all but the red, because these substances are so organized that they respond only to waves of the colors reflected.

Some individuals have the ear so organized that they can hear certain sounds, but are totally deaf to others. The waves of sound strike all tympanums alike; yet in these instances they are incapable of responding to certain waves. Some person who delight in music, although all the lower notes are plainly heard, as soon as the tune rises to a high key, can not hear a single sound. In others, this is reversed. The eye of some individuals is similarly arranged--some colors being undiscernible, while others are perceptible. The vibrations are the same in all these cases, but owing to peculiarities of organization are not felt. As musical instruments to respond must be attuned in harmony, so there must be correlated harmony between minds which transmit and receive thoughts. All minds give out vibrations, as all musical strings give out sounds; and as there must be a corresponding string to receive its notes, so there must be not only a sensitive but harmoniously attuned mind to receive the thought vibrations.

Individuals not mutually harmonious--at least in some point--do not excite a mental influence on each other; but if they are thus organized, they will influence each other. This is unavoidable, whether the will is excited or not; but if the stronger will is exerted, its power is proportionally greater, and it will magnetize the weaker; and the peculiar phenomena attending that mental state will be manifested.

It is not the body which magnetizes or is magnetized; it is the mind; and these effects are produced outside of the physical system. The fact that one person can magnetize another by the simple power of the will, though at a distance, is evidence that the mind in this exercise of power is independent of the body.

If we grant, for the sake of the argument, that there is a spirit back of the physical aspect of mortal life, it will be readily seen that all that has been said of the transference of thought between individuals, holds true between spiritual beings, as this transference at last resides in the spirit-being. As man is a spirit incarnated, differing in that respect only from a disembodied spirit, the body is the only obstacle between him and the spirits above him. Sensitiveness to impressions from another, or from a spirit, rest on the same cause; and in the higher realm of spirit, the transference of thought is controlled by the same laws, and reaches more perfect expression.

Intimations of an Intelligent Force.

BELIEF IN GUARDIAN ANGELS.--Memory brings back the days of our childhood and again we hear our mother sing that simple song of joy, which, it is said, Bishop McKendree murmured on his dying bed:

Bright angels have from glory come, They're round my bed; they're in my room; They wait to waft my spirit home; All is well! All is well!

We approach the dark river of death alone, but we are not to cross without a guide. We may be blind to the light of the celestial sphere in the full pulse of health; we may be insensible to the presence of the nearest and dearest of our departed; yet when death loosens the bonds which unite the physical with the spiritual body, what is known dimly as clairvoyance, the full possession of the spiritual senses, bursts upon the awakened spirit. Then the dying find that death is life, and to leave earthly friends is to meet the hosts of heaven.

That there are guardian angels has been taught from immemorial time, and in some dim form is a belief of all except the lowest races of mankind.

It is a beautiful belief, full of consolation, of assurance, and comfort to the struggling and striving. How hard may press the iron hand of fate, how sharp the flinty stones beneath our bleeding feet, we think of those blessed messengers by our side, and feel that our burdens are for the purpose of giving us strength, else they would turn us aside to more pleasant paths. We know that they are with us in the darkest hours, and enjoy with us the days of our sunshine. We delve in the soil and smirch of the world, and the physical being obscures and overlaps the spiritual to such a degree that our horizon is shut down on that side by thick clouds, and only at long intervals can a ray of light penetrate the darkness.

Our lives might be so well ordered that we would be as conscious of the presence of these guardians as of earthly friends. What is possible at rare moments of lucidity is possible at all times under like conditions. The fault is not on their side, but on ours. The sun forever shines in the heavens, just above the thin vail of clouds, and if the sea does not reflect the starry night, it is because of its agitated surface.

We do not see through the thin vail, which separates the world of spirits and men. We cannot see the air which surges a profound and agitated ocean above and around us. Without material rays of light we could not see material things, and would be practically blind.

If we ascend a mountain in the night, we can only perceive the gray and mossy rocks a few yards ahead of us, bordering the path, beyond which would be impenetrable darkness, gloomy abysses, seemingly unfathomable, and above, the dark night-clouds without a star. On the summit we rest awaiting the morning, seeing nothing, but scenting the faint odors of pine and the fragrance of flowers borne upwards on the gentle air. Patiently we wait until the gray East blushes with a long horizontal line of light flaming upward toward the crimson clouds, and the distant mountain-tops with the silver flood. Lo! the orb of day pushes the clouds aside, and flashes over the world in triumph. What transformation! What grandeur and beauty! Valleys of eden, loveliness at our feet, and snowy summits above our heads! Grand forests clothing the hillsides, bloom and flower everywhere; gem-like lakes, and flashing torrents, endless prospective of mountains on one side, and of plain on the other. All night we were in the midst of this grandeur and beauty, yet saw it not. We seemed suspended between earth and sky, and around us only blackness, yet all this splendor of scenery existed the same as it did before the light made it visible.

Thus the world of spirit may exist around us, unseen, unfelt, except as we perceive the odor of asphodels, or hear the faint murmur of angel whispers, for our eyes are blind to the light, by which it is revealed.

FACTS UNREFERABLE TO PREVIOUSLY CONSIDERED CAUSES.--After referring to hypnotism, somnambulism, clairvoyance and thought transference, a great mass of the facts presented for explanation, there still remain a large number which stand apart by themselves, and which bring an outside or independent intelligence with them, which no exaltation on the part of the actor can supply. The only adequate or even plausible explanation of these facts is that which refers them to the agency of intelligent beings beyond our ken. The presence of such entities may or may not be recognized by the percipient. The ideas and motives may be impressed all the same. We may be assured that unconsciously those who by study and practical experience become adept in particular lines of thought or practical affairs, are the most proper mediums for the communication of spirits dwelling in the same sphere of thought, and that such communications are continuously made unconsciously to the percipients. The weird stories which come up from the rugged toilers of the sea are full of interest in this particular. The infinite solitude of waters; the long and lonely watches, with the sweep of waves and the silent stars, conduce to a state of abstraction and reverie, peculiarly favorable to the reception of impressions. If there is need in this world of the watchful care of guardian angels, the sailor on the lone ship which plows the trackless waste at the mercy of the elements requires them most. Human skill and foresight may provide to the utmost, and yet there remains the greater dangers which can not be foreseen or provided against. The sailor, feeling that he is helpless in the hands of the elements, becomes superstitious, though often what is called in him superstition, is belief in influences which future knowledge may accept as valuable accessions to the realm of mental science. I have from the lips of Capt. D. B. Edwards, the narrative of two incidents in the life of his brother, which illustrates this faculty of intuition, if we may give it that name; and if one were to gather up similar stories which are told by the officers, volumes might be filled.

Capt. John B. Edwards was in command of the steamship "Monterey," one of the New York and New Orleans line of steamers. In one of his voyages he came up with Sandy Hook in a terrible storm. The air was so full of driving snow that the officers could not see the length of the vessel. The sea was high and rapidly increasing, and no pilot responded. To remain was impossible; to go on was almost certain destruction. If the Captain could make the light-ship he would know his bearings, and be able to steer into harbor; but in that drift of blinding snow and rush of waters, in which he had made his approach from the sea, he had been unable to make observations, and had no assurance that he had not deviated from his course under the influence of the drift of wind or current, at least to the variation of a league or more. In his perplexity he ordered the ship to be stopped, and for a moment reflected on the difficulties of his position. While thus waiting, with every sense strained to the utmost, an impression came like a flash, that the light-ship lay in a certain direction. He immediately ordered the officers to keep a sharp lookout forward, for he would run ten minutes in a certain direction to test his impression. The great wheels again revolved, and the steamer swung obedient to command, and rushed on into the drift. In six minutes the mate on the bow threw up his hands, crying: "Hard-a-port! hard-a-port!" and the steamer quickly responding to her helm, passed the stern of the light-ship, from which the Captain easily took his bearings and safely steamed into the port of New York.

During the war Capt. Edwards was coast pilot for the Government steamer "Vanderbilt." During one voyage he came up to the "Hook;" a storm was coming on and no pilot in sight. The Commodore came to the wheel-house and asked Capt. Edwards if he thought he could take the ship into port. Edwards shrank and trembled at the question, for he knew the ship was drawing as much, if not more water, than was on the bar, and the responsibility thus thrust upon him was overwhelming. But suddenly he was forced to speak, replying without hesitation: "Yes, sir." "Go ahead," was the order of the Commodore. With every faculty intensely active, his strong and steady hand held the wheel, and the ship went over the bar without touching, and all was well. His ability and trustworthiness for the action received the highest recommendation from the Commodore.

It is sad to learn that this noble man sacrificed his own life in caring for his mate, who was a victim of yellow fever in the hospital of Rio Janeiro. From the many remarkable experiences in his own life, Capt. D. B. Edwards related, I take one which is characteristic of the others. He is a strong and powerfully built man, with every line indicative of honest resolution and endurance. He has retired from the sea-faring life, but has made his home by the coast. He impresses one with rare and sterling honesty and purity of character, and a self-contained repose which is a peculiarity of most officers who have passed their lives at sea.

He said that one bright day in March, sailing up Long Island, he was overtaken by a snow-storm which suddenly concealed all landmarks, and the wind momentarily increasing, soon became a terrific gale. In that narrow strait one has not to sail for a great length of time in the wrong direction to reach the coast. As night came on the situation became more appalling, and wreck most certain. He gave the wheel to the mate and allowed himself time to reflect. He could arrive at no conclusion. Suddenly it flashed through his mind to steer by the lead! How? "Why, where the Thames enters the Sound it is deeper. When you reach that channel follow it into safety." It was the only chance, and he seized it. He went to the bow, for he would trust no one, ordering the mate to implicitly, and with utmost readiness, obey orders, and hold the vessel on her present course. Standing at the bow, with the spray falling in torrents over him, and the wind straining the spars to the utmost, he cast the lead to find the ordinary level of the Sound. He continued to cast until suddenly deeper water was indicated, and with joy he gave the order that changed the course of the vessel, and in a few minutes brought her into the still waters of the Thames. Then, he said, in a change of warm, dry clothing, they sat in the snug cabin and drank their hot coffee with a sense of peace words can but feebly express.

SAVED FROM DEATH BY A PREMONITION.--It may be said that under the stimulus of danger and great emergency, the mental faculties become intensified, and that we can not fix their limits; that all that was required of Capt. Edwards was courage to act in response to knowledge he had acquired, but which was latent until called forth by the extraordinary demand. We shall now introduce facts to which this pleading will not apply. The first shows two distinct intelligences, one of which was superior to that of mortals, for it could foresee the future, and must have acted on Capt. McGowan, to compel him to relinquish a well formed plan, without any assignable reason, and pursue one entirely different. The thought of the theater had not entered his mind, and he gave his boys no excuse for breaking his word with them.

Capt. McGowan, 12th U. S. I., thus relates this story (J. S. P. R., Feb., 1885):

"In Jan. 1887, I was on leave of absence in Brooklyn, with my two boys, then on a vacation from school. I promised to take them to the theater that night and engaged seats for us three. At the same time I had an opportunity to examine the interior of the theater, and went over it carefully, stage and all. These seats were engaged on the previous day, but on the day of the proposed visit it seemed as if a voice within me was constantly saying, 'Do not go to the theater; take the boys back to school.' I could not keep these words out of my mind; they grew stronger and stronger, and at noon I told my friends and the boys I would not go to the theater. My friends remonstrated with me, and said I was cruel to deprive the boys of a promised and unfamiliar pleasure, and I partially relented; but all the afternoon the words kept repeating themselves and impressing themselves upon me. That evening, less than an hour before the doors opened, I insisted on the boys going to New York with me, and spending the night at a hotel convenient to the railroad, by which we could start in the early morning. I felt ashamed of the feeling which impelled me to act thus, but there seemed no escape from it. That night the theater was destroyed by fire, with the loss of 300 lives. Had I been present, from my previous examination of the building, I should certainly have taken my children over the stage when the fire broke out, in order to escape by a private exit, and would just as certainly have been lost as were all those who trusted to it, for that passage by an accident could not be used.... I never had a presentiment before nor since. What was it that caused me, against my desire, to abandon the play after having secured the seats and carefully arranged for the pleasure?"

SAVED FROM INTEMPERANCE.--S. H. Mann, of Washington, D. C., wrote the following personal experience to Dr. M. L. Holbrook. When a youth, he was clerk in a country store, and formed the habit of saturating loaf sugar with brandy and eating it. It was in the early part of this century, and before the temperance movement had been inaugurated. At that time the use of alcoholic beverages was considered almost as essential to health as food. He had regarded the saturated sugar as a pleasant confection and had not become aware of the strong hold the habit had taken on him, or how passionately fond of it he had become. One day he went into the cellar with his sugar, saturated it, and was in the act of raising it to his mouth, when his arm became paralyzed, and a voice out of the air, for he was alone, spoke to him in stern tones, saying: "Young man, stop! If you continue this habit you will die a drunkard!" He could not move his hand to his mouth, and at last he let the sugar drop as his hand fell helpless by his side. The occurrence made such a strong impression on him, that he became a total abstainer, at a time when nearly all drank, and has remained true to his convictions all his life.

A SOLDIER'S LIFE SAVED BY A DREAM.--This story is yet more remarkable. Rev. L. W. Lewis, in his "Reminiscences of the War," published in the Christian Advocate, relates an instance where a dream saved the life of a soldier: "A man by the name of Williams had told a dream to his fellow-soldiers, some of whom related it to me months previous to the occurrence which I now relate. He dreamed that he crossed a river, marched over a mountain and camped near a church located in a wood, near which a terrible battle ensued, and in a charge just as we crossed the ravine he was shot in the heart. On the ever memorable 7th of December, 1862 (Battle of Prairie Grove, Northern Arkansas), as we moved at double-quick to take our places in the line of battle, then already hotly engaged, we passed the church, a small frame building. I was riding in the flank of the command opposite to Williams, as we came in view of the house. 'That is the church I saw in my dream,' said he. I made no reply, and never thought of the matter again until the evening. We had broken the enemy's lines and were in full pursuit, when we came to a dry ravine in the wood; and Williams said: 'Just on the other side of this ravine I was shot in my dream, and I'll stick my hat under my shirt.' Suiting the action to the word he doubled up his hat as he ran along and crammed it into his bosom. Scarcely had he adjusted it when a Minie ball knocked him out of line; jumping up quickly he pulled out his hat, waved it over his head shouting, 'I'm all right!' The ball raised a black spot, about the size of a man's hand, just over his heart, and dropped into his shoe."

Here the prophecy was a long time ahead, and foretold the exact coming of a ball depending on a combination of circumstances which would seem impossible for reason or intuition to foresee and foreknow. Its fulfillment was peculiar, for by guarding against it, the danger was averted and the dream proved untrue.

AN ERROR CORRECTED IN A REMARKABLE MANNER.--The head bookkeeper in one of the largest sewing machine companies in New York City, in balancing his books found an error of $5.00. It was a small sum, but as a mistake was as damaging as $500. He set his assistants at work to find it, yet day after day their labor was in vain. They worked for a week and accomplished nothing. He became greatly annoyed and filled with anxiety. In his own words: "The third Sunday after the search was begun, I got up late after a sleepless night and started out on a walk for exercise. My mind was on my books, and I paid no attention to the direction I took. My surprise was, therefore, genuine when I found myself at the door of the company's office in Union Square, for I had not certainly intended to go there. Mechanically I put my hand in my pocket, drew out the key, opened the door and went in. As if in a dream I walked to the office, where I turned the combination and unlocked the safe. There were the books, a dozen of them in a row. I did not consider for a moment which to take up. It was by no volition on my part that my hand moved toward a certain one, and drew it from the safe. Placing it on the desk, I opened it; my eye ran along the column of figures, and there before me, plain as day, was the missing $5.00. I made a note of the page, put the book back in the safe, and went home. It was then noon. I lay down and fell into a deep sleep from which I did not awake until nine o'clock on Monday morning. After a hearty breakfast I hastened to the office feeling like a new man. It seemed as if a burden had fallen from me, and I was walking on air."

This bookkeeper, by anxiety and overwork, had become very sensitive. He was by the account he gives of himself, in a state bordering on clairvoyance. He was automatically used, not by a "dominant idea," for the dominant idea caused his mistake, and that could not suggest to him the book and page, which were readily found by his hand being moved by some cause. As the hand could not move itself, it must have been acted on by an intelligent, independent force.

A MOTHER SAVES THE LIFE OF HER SON.--Of warnings there are no end, and, however much the truth of prophecy may be denied, it is certain that within at least narrow bounds future events may be foretold. One instance of this being correctly done may be referred to coincidence, but two places the probabilities on the other side, and three makes it impossible. It will be readily comprehended that no guess told the soldier a ball would strike him at a certain time and place, or the father that the theater would be burned on a certain night.

There is a series of facts which show direct interposition of superior intelligence, of which the following may be taken as examples. Col. Walter B. Daulay gives his personal experience when on shipboard the "Gulf of Lyons" in a gale of wind:

"I had the mid watch. The night was dark and terrible, the wind howled furiously and the heaving sea tossed our ship about like a bit of cork. I stood by the mizzen mast, holding on by the fife-rail, and shielding my face from the blinding spray that came driving over the deck. Suddenly I heard my name pronounced as distinctly as I ever heard it in my life--'Walter! Walter!' and it was my mother's voice that spoke. She continued to call me from the gloom about the main mast, and without stopping to reflect, or thinking where I was, I leaped forward. Hardly had I reached the after-companion-way, when I heard a crash behind me, and was called to myself. I turned and found that an iron-banded burton-block had fallen from the top and struck the deck exactly where I had been standing! Had I remained by the fife-rail three seconds longer than I did, my brains would have been dashed out. I always regarded that as an interposition in my behalf of a power independent of human will."

DEATH FORETOLD IN A VISION.--The following facts are vouched for by S. Bigelow, a gentleman of unquestioned integrity and a shrewd observer. In the early days of our war one Albert Dexter, near Ionia, Mich., enlisted in Co. D, Third Michigan Cavalry. His sister, Mrs. John Dunham, living then and now in Ionia, had what she terms a vision the day before he enlisted in which she saw him--her brother Albert--on horseback; saw him wheel and fall from his horse. She told Albert of her vision and importuned him not to go, but he made light of her fears and vision, and went with his company to the fields of blood and carnage, and often in his letters he referred to his sister's fears and vision in a light and joyful mood; but in his last letter he seemed to believe in the vision and in its probable fulfillment. More than two years had passed since the vision, and no unfavorable news from Albert, when one afternoon in autumn, as Mrs. Dunham was alone in her quiet home, she heard a loud rap at the door, opened it, saw no one, felt impressed, and queried with herself, "Why can't they tell me?" but could get nothing definite beyond her impressions, and the plain, loud rap about which she could not be mistaken. But during the quiet hours of night her spiritual vision was quickened, and she saw Albert on horseback, advance, then wheel, and then saw him shot and fall, and as plainly as though she had been by his side. She saw just where he was hit, how he fell, etc. Hence she knew all, having full confidence in such manifestations, as they were not new to her.

She suffered intense agony and a sleepless night, not expecting herself to survive; was pale and haggard in the morning, and scarcely able to be up. She told her friends and family about the matter in detail, even to the writing of a letter by the lieutenant informing them. She gave the contents of the letter before it was written. This was on Tuesday night and following morning. The next Sunday Mrs D. was visiting six miles from Ionia, and during the day a messenger came bringing a letter, which John Dexter had just received from the lieutenant of the Third Michigan Cavalry, giving particulars of his brother Albert's death while engaged in action the previous Tuesday, confirming in every detail what Mrs. D. had seen and told; and farther, she felt or saw the messenger with the letter while yet far from the house, and told him what he had, and gave the contents of the letter, assuring him that it was no news to her.

Another brother, James, enlisted and went to the war, and one evening as Mrs. D. was in bed and Mr. D. was reading, they both heard plainly the report of a pistol (or what seemed to them such), and Mrs. D. saw Albert and James come in and fall near her bed, and told Mr. D. that James was dead, which was fully confirmed by letter in about two weeks.

THE ASSASSINATION OF GARFIELD PREDICTED.--The assassination of Garfield was foretold by many sensitives, for that great event seemed to cast a strong shadow before it. Several of these prophecies have been published since the event, and consequently have lost their weight as evidence, while others had been widely published before the terrible tragedy. The following rests on the integrity of S. Bigelow, and is unquestionably true.

A gentleman in Cleveland, O., well known there, saw and knew that Garfield would be assassinated long before he left his quiet Mentor home, and was so oppressed with the knowledge that he told Mayor Rose and Dr. Streator, two very prominent and wealthy friends of Garfield, and both active politicians as well, and they conferred with others, and finally wrote to Garfield about it; but the sensitive, in the meantime, felt impelled to do something, and that he must go and see Garfield and warn him, but being a stranger and in humble circumstances he thought he could not go; but he could get no peace until he did, and finally plucked up courage to undertake the, to him, dreaded mission, and went alone and sad, to Mentor. Garfield met him in person (not by secretary as he did others) at the door, and greeted him cordially, and thus enabled him to overcome his embarrassment in a measure, and to talk freely, which he did, and as a consequence Garfield's bed was moved from his bedroom on the lower floor to the chamber.

This precaution prevented the crime for a time, which was ripe for execution. The same gentleman felt impelled to go to Washington with the fateful vision, but was prevented from going, and thus unwarned, Garfield met his death.

OMENS.--Almost every one has good and bad omens, and although they may think that they have entirely outgrown such superstition, they will find that there yet lingers more or less of the feeling from education or heredity. They do not believe that seeing the moon over the left shoulder indicates bad luck, and over the right good fortune, yet they would prefer to see it over the right. They do not think Friday a more unlucky day than the other six, yet avoid commencing important business on that day. There are a great number of omens and signs, many of them peculiar to the individual; others worldwide, and held from remote antiquity. Of these it may be said that while of themselves these signs and omens have no relation to the events they presage, if we suppose a person to accept a certain omen as foreshadowing a certain event, a superior being foreknowing that event and desiring to impress it on the mind of such person, might use the sign to convey the warning. To further illustrate: There may be no connection between seeing the moon over one's right shoulder and a fortunate event in store; but a superior being, foreseeing that event, may so influence our minds as to make us catch a glimpse of the crescent on the right.

Mrs. Bancroft, a daughter-in-law of the great historian, has described an uncanny circumstance which happened at a wedding in 1863, where the wives of Major Thos. Y. Brent and Capt. Eugene Barnes, of the C. S. A. met, each wearing her bridal dress. While dressing for the occasion, Mrs. Brent's companion discovered a blood spot upon the dress of the Major's wife, which could not be accounted for, and somewhat excitedly exclaimed: "It is a bad omen!" Two days after, Mrs. Brent experienced a severe pain in the region of her heart, although at the time in the best of health. This occurred at the birth-place of her husband. Two days later she heard that while storming a Federal fortification, her husband was killed on July 4th, 1863, as far as she could learn at the identical time that she experienced the heart-pain. The Major was shot in the breast by a Minie ball and instantly killed. Another fact occurred at the time of finding the blood spot, and that was Mrs. Thomas Bright addressing the two ladies as "war widows." She believes in omens, and believes that these facts pointed to the death of the lady's husband, which occurred so soon after.

A DREAM REALIZED.--The Mobile Register published the following, under the title of "A Dream Realized," which should be regarded as a trance, in which state the transcendent knowledge was given by some superior intelligence:

"A man named Bronson, who was an agent for a seed house, was travelling through Tennessee making collections. One night, after he had finished his business in Chattanooga, he made ready for a horseback ride of fifteen or twenty miles the next day. Upon retiring to his room for the night he sat down to smoke a cigar.

"He was neither overtired nor sleepy, but, after smoking a few minutes, he had what he termed a vision. He was riding over the country on horseback; when at the junction of two roads he was joined by a stranger. He saw this man as plainly as one man can see another in broad daylight, noting the color of his hair and eyes and taking particular notice of the fact that the horse, which was gray in color, had a "y" branded on his left shoulder.

"The two rode along together for a mile or more, and then came to a spot where a tree had been blown down and fallen across the narrow highway. They turned into the woods to pass the spot, he in advance, when he saw the stranger pull a pistol and fire at his back. He felt the bullet tear into him, reeled and fell from his horse, and was conscious when the assassin robbed him and drew his body further into the woods. He seemed to see all this, and yet at the same time knew that he was dead. His corpse was rolled into a hollow and covered with brush, and then the murderer went away and left him alone.

"In making an effort to throw off the brush, he awoke. His cigar had gone out, and, as near as he could calculate, he had been unconscious, as you might call it, for about fifteen minutes. He was deeply agitated, and it was some time before he could convince himself that he had not suffered any injury. By-and-by he went to bed and slept soundly, and next morning the remembrance of what had happened in his vision had almost faded from his mind.

"He set out on his journey in good spirits, and found the road so romantic, and met horsemen going to town so often, that he reached the junction of the roads without having given a serious thought to his vision.

"Then every circumstance was recalled in the most vivid manner.

"He was joined there by a stranger on a gray horse, and man and beast tallied exactly with those in the vision. The man did not, however, have the look or bearing of an evil-minded person. On the contrary, he seemed to be in a jolly mood, and he saluted Bronson as frankly as an honest stranger would have done. He had no weapons in sight, and he soon explained that he was going to the village to which Bronson was bound, on business connected with the law.

"The agent could not help but feel astonished and startled at the curious coincidence, but the stranger was so talkative and friendly that there was no possible excuse to suspect him. Indeed, as if to prove to his companion that he meditated no evil, he kept a little in advance for the next half hour. Bronson's distrust had entirely vanished, when a turn in the road brought an obstruction to view. There was a fallen tree across the highway! This proof that every point and circumstance in the vision was being unrolled before his eyes, gave the agent a great shock. He was behind the stranger, and he pulled out his revolver and dropped his hand beside the horse to conceal it.

"'Well, well!' said the man, as he pulled up his horse; 'the tree must have toppled over this morning. We'll have to pass around it to the right.'

"Bronson was on the right. The woods were clear of underbrush, and, naturally enough, he should have been the first to leave the road, but he waited.

"'Go ahead, friend,' said the stranger, as if the words had been addressed to the horse; the animal which the agent bestrode started up.

"Bronson was scarcely out of the road before he turned in his saddle. The stranger had a pistol in his right hand. What followed could not be clearly related. Bronson slid from the saddle as a bullet whizzed past him, and a second later returned the fire. Three or four shots were rapidly exchanged, and then the would-be murderer, uttering a yell showing that he had been hit, wheeled his horse to gallop off. He had not gone ten rods when the beast fell under him, and he kicked his feet from the stirrups and sprang into the woods and was out of sight in a moment. The horse had received a bullet in the throat and was dead in a few minutes."

A YOUNG LADY'S DREAM.--Miss Amelia Ederly, young lady highly endowed, both mentally and physically, and free from superstition or inclination to the marvelous, while visiting friends one evening shortly before her death, related a dream which she had a few days previous, which had vividly impressed itself on her mind. She thought she saw herself ready for burial, with her parents and friends weeping around her. She had no feeling; only surprise that her body was clothed with a blue dress with yellow roses, and she attempted to expostulate at this want of taste, but no one gave attention to her remarks. She jested about the dream, and it seemed not to make any deep impression; but ten days after this visit she was taken sick and died. She had mentioned her dream only once, and her sickness could not be referred to mental impression received thereby.

A WARNING VOICE.--Dr. Fisher, of Waterford, England, is authority for the following:

"Miss Louisa Benn, who lived with her mother in Wednesbury, had become desirous of going to Australia; her friends assisted her to means. After she had made preparations, she left her home for London, and secured passage on a ship. On the day before the sailing of the ship her mother heard a cry of, 'Oh, mother,' seemingly from the cellar, and in her daughter's voice. She was so alarmed that she telegraphed for her daughter to return, which she reluctantly did, for she was already on board, and her luggage being stored away, could not be given her. Her regret vanished when news came that the vessel was lost, and with it nearly all the passengers."

AN OBJECTION.--Here arises an objection often urged against such premonitions. Of an hundred or more of passengers, one only is warned, while all the others are allowed to go on board and blindly meet their fate. If such warning come from God, with whom all things are possible, the objection would have pertinence, and be unanswerable unless relegated to the mystery of Godliness. But such warnings do not come from God, but from spirit intelligences just above ourselves, departed friends who preserve an interest in those who remain on earth. It is not probable that all, or even any considerable portion of these intelligences, are able to forecast the future, or possess the equally essential ability to impress their thoughts on their earthly friends. The few who know the events of the future may find it impossible to communicate with their friends. Hence the rare occurrence of such premonitions, and the strange spectacle of only a single individual among hundreds receiving intimations of approaching danger. Thus where the laws and conditions of impressibility are understood, it is not anomalous that so few are impressed, but this fact confirms the theory of sensitiveness.

Premonitions and presentiments of coming events form a numerous class of well attested cases. They usually relate directly to the person receiving them, and those recorded in a majority of instances refer to sickness or death. It may be supposed that a great majority of premonitions received, are not recognized, or at least recorded. Many by reception defeat their fulfillment, quite as many, probably, as bring their fulfillment by being received. When an individual has a premonition that he is to die at a certain time, and does thus die, it is said the prophecy so worked on his mind that it killed him at the appointed time. Possibly this might happen, but it rarely does. Far more often the knowledge prepares for the event, and the individual survives to point at the prophecy as a failure. Again, the presentiment comes with the certainty of a decree of fate, and the future is without shadow of turning, and inexorable to our efforts or our prayers.

ABRAHAM LINCOLN'S DREAM.--The following dream by Abraham Lincoln is a matter of history, and is in harmony with the susceptible nature of that great man. He related it to Mrs. Lincoln and others present in the following words:

"About ten days ago I retired very late. I had been up waiting for important dispatches. I could not have been long in bed, when I fell into a slumber and began to dream. There seemed to be a death-like stillness about me. Then I heard subdued sobs, as if a number of persons were weeping. I thought I left my bed and wandered down stairs. There the silence was broken by the same sobbing, but the mourners were invisible. I went from room to room. No living person was in sight, but the same mournful sounds met me as I passed along. I was puzzled and alarmed. What could be the meaning of all this? Determined to find out the cause of a state of things so mysterious, I kept on until I arrived at the 'end room,' which I entered. There I met a sickening surprise. Before me was a catafalque, on which rested a corpse wrapped in funeral vestments. Around it were stationed soldiers who were acting as guards; and there was a throng of people, some gazing mournfully upon this corpse, whose face was covered; others weeping pitifully, 'Who is dead at the White House?' I demanded of one of the soldiers. 'The President,' was his answer; 'he was killed by an assassin!' Then came a loud burst of grief from the crowd, which awoke me from my dream. I slept no more that night; and although it was only a dream, I have been strangely annoyed by it ever since."

This occurred but a short time before the event it heralded, which plunged the nation into grief. Had the President given heed to its warning, and not been persuaded by his wife, who gave no credit to the supernatural, the course of events would have been different. Had he heeded the dream it would have been brought forward as evidence to prove the worthlessness of such visions.

A LITTLE GIRL PREDICTS HER OWN DEATH.--Little Maud, three-year-old daughter of George T. Ford, of Elmore, Mich., came to her mother one day and said, "Maudie is not going to stay; she is going away off to be buried up in the cold ground." About a week later, she said, "Let Maudie go and ride with you to-day, for she will never go again." On the morning of the day of her death, she came to her mother and said, "Maudie don't feel well. Don't you feel sorry for Maudie? She is going away off where you will never see her again." Her mother clasped her to her bosom, wondering what she could mean, but was not long left in doubt. The child grew seriously ill, and later in the day she said, "Good-bye--lift me up--I hear the band playing--I am going now," and passed away.

PRINCE LEOPOLD'S DREAM.--Another instance, important in consequence of the noble station of the person to whom it relates, is given in the Fortnightly Review, by W. H. Myers:

"The last time I saw Prince Leopold (being two days before he died), he would talk to me about death, and said he would like a military funeral.

"Finally I asked, 'why do you talk in this morose manner?' As he was about to answer, he was called away and said, 'I will tell you later.' I never saw him to speak to again, but he finished his answer to me to a lady, and said: 'Two nights now, Princess Alice has appeared to me in my dreams, and says she is quite happy and wants me to come and join her; that is what makes me so very thoughtful.'

"I take this to be a sign of his approaching removal to the world of spirits, in which, as a member of a Spiritualistic family, he has been, from his earliest youth, an implicit believer, thus illustrating the truth of the observation, that, 'Signs are vouchsafed to the believing, now, as of old.'"

ANOTHER CASE.--Miss Mary Paine, when on her way to visit some friends in Gainesville, Ga., on passing the Mars Hill Graveyard, ordered her driver to stop the team, which he did. Then she exacted a promise from him that he would bring her back and bury her by the side of her sister Jane. "For," said she, "I shall never come back alive. I shall die away from home, and I want you to promise to bring me back for burial." To this declaration she clung, nor would she be persuaded that, as she was in good health she would have a pleasant visit and return home happy. Before three weeks had passed she died of a congestive chill, at her friend's house in Gainesville, and as she had requested, was brought back to Mars Hill and buried by the side of her dear sister.

Dr. H----, who is of exceedingly skeptical organization, said that he once had an experience which baffled his powers of explanation, and caused him to doubt his materialistic views. He had been called to a distant farm-house on an intensely dark and stormy night to visit a patient. There was a stream with wide marshy borders, across which a narrow causeway had been constructed, barely wide enough for carriages to pass. As he drove onto one end of this narrow way, suddenly there came the thought that he would meet a runaway team, and his horse and carriage be overturned into the morass. At that time of night this was wholly improbable; but the thought came to him instantly with all its contingencies. "If I should meet a team, what shall I do?" he asked himself. Then he thought there was one place wider than the rest, and he answered, "I would reach that place and get as far out of the way as possible." "Get there, then; get there," was the urgent impression. He involuntarily hurried his horse, reached the place, and, driving to the very edge, drew rein. He was in a tremor of nervous excitement, yet had seen nor heard nothing to excite him more than the interior impression. But he soon found his haste had not been in vain. He heard the rattle of wheels and clatter of hoofs, as a runaway team struck the further end of the causeway, and in a moment they swept past him. Had they met him unprepared, he certainly would have met with a serious, if not fatal, accident. This intelligence which saw the approaching team and the great danger in which Dr. H. would be placed, was independent of his mind, for it brought a knowledge that mind did not, nor could not know until revealed by some foreign power. Whence came the premonition, the thoughtful care? Not out of the air. It was from an intelligent, individualized entity above and beyond physical existence; and all theories which leave out this element fall short of covering the multitudinous facts which unite and bind them together in a harmonious whole.

SEEN AT HIS FUNERAL.--Dr. John E. Purdon, now of Valley Head, Ala., is authority for the following narrative, which records the appearance of a soldier soon after his death, and may be taken as evidence of the sensitiveness on one side, and of the reality of the existence of the appearance on the other:

"In the year 1872, while in charge of the convalescent hospital, Sandown,

Isle of Wight, I returned from a short visit to London, bringing with me for change and rest Miss Florence Cook, who afterwards became so celebrated a medium. On the evening of my return home, I took a walk with Miss Cook along the cliffs towards Shanklin. During the walk she drew my attention to a soldier who seemed to her to be behaving in a curious way, turning round and staring at me, and omitting the usual military salute which she had noticed the other men give as they passed by. As I could see no one at the time my curiosity was excited, and when she said the man had passed a stile just in front of us, I crossed over and looked carefully about. No soldier was in sight; on one side was an open field; on the other, perpendicular cliffs. I asked a country man at work in the field if he had seen a soldier pass just before I appeared, but he had not.

"On my return from town I found that a certain chronic patient who had been a long time in the hospital, and on whom I had performed a minor surgical operation some time before, had died of pulmonary consumption.

"Miss Cook and another young lady on a visit to my wife, never having seen a military funeral, persuaded her to take them to a cross-road, where they would see the troops pass without being seen themselves. As we marched past, the coffin being carried on a gun-carriage, Miss Cook said to my wife, 'Why is the little man in front dressed differently from the other soldier?' My wife answered that she could not see any one in front, nor could the other girl either. Miss Cook then said, 'Why does he not wear a big hat like the others? He has on a small cap and is holding his head down.' They then returned home, and the funeral party passed on to the graveyard which was two miles from the hospital. Just after the firing party had fallen in to march home, Hospital Sergeant Malandine came up to me in the graveyard and said: 'Private Edwards reports sick, sir, and asks permission to return by train.' I asked what was the matter, and the sergeant answered that Edwards had had a great fright from seeing the man we were burying looking down into his own grave at the coffin before it was covered by the clay!"

APPEARANCE AFTER DEATH.--Light, a journal that exercises great discretion in the facts it publishes, vouches for the following appearance coincident with death, received from Mr. F. J. Teall:

"In the year 1884 my son Walter was serving in the Soudan, in the 3d King's

Royal Rifles. The last we heard from him was a letter informing us that he expected to return to England about Christmas time. On October 24th I returned home in the evening, and noticing my wife looking very white, I said, 'What is the matter with you?' She said she had seen Walter, and he had stooped down to kiss her, but, owing to her starting, he was gone; so she did not receive the kiss. He was in his regimentals, and she thought he had come on furlough, to take her by surprise, knowing the back way; but when she saw he was gone and the door not open, she became dreadfully frightened. My son Frederick and daughters Selina and Nellie were in the room, but none of them saw Walter; only Fred heard his mother scream, 'Oh!' and asked her what was the matter.

"I thought, having heard many tales of this kind, that I would jot it down, so I put the date on a slip of paper. After that we had a letter from the lady nurse of the Ramleh Hospital, in Egypt, to say that the poor boy had suffered a third relapse of enteric fever. They thought that he would have pulled through, but he was taken. When we got the letter it was a week after he died; but the date when the letter was written corresponded with the day Walter appeared, which was on October 24th, 1884. My wife never got over the shock, but brooded over it, and finally died April 29th, 1886, of mental derangement."

FOREWARNING.--Miss Lena Harman, as reported in the Globe-Democrat, is authority for a most instructive narrative of ghastly interference in the affairs of men, which forms another link in the chain of evidence showing that there is a spirit-world interested in the events of this. Miss Harman was a warm friend of Mrs. Lena Reich, who was foully murdered by her husband in New York. She had not seen her for several months prior to her death, but the last time she met her, Mrs. Reich told her a pitiful story of her husband's abuse, and said she ought not to have married him for she had been forewarned. She had been obliged to have him bound over to keep the peace, and knew he would yet kill her. The warning came before she was married, even before their engagement. In her own words it happened this way. "Adolph had been courting me for some time, and I knew that I loved him. One night, a terrible dark, storming winter night, he told me that he loved me, and offered himself to me. I acknowledged that I was not indifferent to him, but asked a few days to think over the matter and consult my friends. Adolph did not like this delay, and tried to reason me out of it, but I was firm and carried my point. Well, we sat up very late that night together, no one else but ourselves being in the room. When he finally left it was past midnight, and the weather was very cold, so I fixed up the fire to make me a cup of tea to quiet my nerves, and warm me up before going to bed. I was a little sorry I had been so positive to Adolph about the time, as I loved him and I thought I might as well say yes, any way, so that he would have gone home so much happier.

"As I poured out my cup of tea I said aloud to myself, 'Yes, I love Adolph.' Just then I heard a noise on the stairs, and, thinking some one was going by my door, I turned off the gas, because I did not want any one to know I was keeping such late hours. As the fire in the stove gave out a ruddy light, and the half-darkness of the room seemed so peaceful, and suited my mood of mind so well, I did not light the gas again, but sat and sipped my tea in the darkness, saying little things to myself aloud. Suddenly, however, I heard a slight noise behind me, and at the same time I heard a church clock, strike the hour of one. Well, I looked around without a thought of anything strange, and saw my Ernest, to whom I had been previously engaged, and who died before the ceremony, almost at the altar. He was dressed in the same clothes as when I saw him last--his wedding suit--for we were going to our wedding when he died of heart disease.

"I shrieked and tried to fly from my room, but he spoke: 'Do not move, Lena; I will not harm you. I come because I love you, and because I pity you. Lena, if you marry Adolph Reich you will lead the life of a dog. He will be cruel and jealous, and unreasonable, and, worse than all, he will murder you in the end. Yes, he will murder you! Stay! I see the scene now! He grasps your hair; he holds a sharp carving knife in the other hand; you reach out for the knife and seize it, when, with a terrible oath, he draws the keen blade out of your grasp, and almost severs your fingers in doing so! Oh! he has you down on the bed; he draws the knife; you struggle and scream. He strikes the blade into your neck!--your beautiful neck; you struggle more violently and escape. With the blood spurting from your wound, you run from the room and fall in the hall; and the villain escapes, carrying the knife with him! Oh, terrible! terrible!' Then there was a silence; Ernest said no more for some minutes, and I was too much horrified to speak; but again he said: 'Lena, I love you as much as I ever did, and it won't be long now before you join me here, and we shall be happy again. Oh, do not marry Reich, as you value your life and soul! Farewell! God keep you!' and he was gone!"

The warning was fulfilled to the letter. After the infliction of the terrible wound which caused her death; she had crawled out of her room, and fell in the hall from the loss of blood. How many similar warnings pass unheeded, and yet how greatly might the recipients be benefited by heeding them!

Effects of Physical Influences on the Sensitive.

Individuals who are influenced to an unusual extent by their surroundings, are regarded as nervous,--a name covering a multitude of ills for which no other term is at command. A cat entering the room, however stealthily, in some awakes the most disagreeable feelings. Another is so sensitive to the electric state of the weather as to presage the coming storm several hours or days in advance. Sunday is so called because of its supposed connection with the phases of the moon. The superstitious observation of the Signs arises from the dull understanding or ignorance of this influence. That man is a magnet, and has polarity corresponding to that of the earth, is a plausible conjecture, which receives confirmation by the influence of the earth currents on many forms of disease. Some patients are so exceedingly sensitive that they can lie at ease in no other position than with their heads to the north; and it has been argued that if such position is best for the sensitive it is for all.

More especially is the influence of physical forces seen when death occurs after a lingering disease, which, by reducing the bodily strength, makes that of the spirit more susceptible.

"He's going out with the tide," is the common expression of all the rough coastwise people. It may be called a superstition of sea-faring races; but it is a fact that for some inscrutable reason the old, sick and infirm more often die at the ebb-tide than when the tide is rising. A poet beautifully expresses this belief:

"When the tide goes out he will pass away, Pray for a soul's serene release! That the weary spirit may rest in peace, When the tide goes out."

A physician on the Connecticut coast, who had made special observations, said: "for more than thirty years I have lived and observed among the rough, hardy souls hereabout; and for more than fifty my father before me gathered facts and wisdom from practice. I have stood by hundreds of death-beds of fishermen and farmers, old and young, during the last quarter of a century; but I can hardly recall a single instance of a person dying of disease, who did not pass away while the tide was ebbing. It is a fact that in critical cases I never feel concerned to leave a patient for an hour or two when the tide is coming in; but when it is receding, and particularly in the latter stages of the ebb, I stay by, if I can, till the turn comes. You'll scarcely credit it, but the daily record of the tides is the most important part of the almanac in my practice. If a patient who is very low lives to see the current turn from ebb to flow, I know the case is safe till the ebb sets in again."

"When the tide comes in death waits for dole, When the tide ebbs it takes a soul."

Francis Gerry Fairchild says that during five years he noted the hour and minute of ninety-three demises, and of these all but four (who died of accidents) went out with the ebb of the tide. In his own words: "I who have sat with my fingers on the wrist of many a feeble patient, and noticed the pulse rise and strengthen, or sink and vanish, with the turning of the tide, know that it is fact."

Of twenty-one cases of death registered on the sea coast of Long Island at Orient, by Capt. D. B. Edwards, I find, by careful examination, that with only one exception, the aged, or those who had been suffering from long sickness, died at the ebb of the tide. Those cases were taken as they came, and afford an average that may be depended upon.

Not that the coming and going of the ocean wave as it rolls round the world has special influence. The cause is more profound, and blended with the force of gravitation. Not only is the ocean agitated and piled up beneath the moon; the deeper and more elastic aerial sea is more strongly fluctuated, and the electric and magnetic conditions change with certain periodicity. The maximum of positive force is attained at high tide, constantly increasing as the tide comes in, and then recedes to the zero of negativeness with its outgoing. With the flood of water, and higher pressure of atmosphere, the forces of life are stimulated by the increasing positiveness. When these stimulants withdraw, the tide runs to the negative pole, and a soul ebbs from the mortal shore. Man is sensitive to the influences of the sun and moon, and to the stars.

The influence of the moon in cases of lunacy has been observed from ancient times, and a lunar month measures the cycle of changes in most cases of madness.

During health these subtle changes are not felt, or too feebly to be remarked. It is during sickness, when the physical energies are so enfeebled that slight forces turn the balance for or against, that the most palpable effects are produced. There are moon-tides and sun-tides in the ocean and in the air. Sometimes these augment, at others depress each other. The magnetic disturbances are much greater at times than others; hence the subject is complicated; but when investigated it will be shown that there is co-operation between vital force and the energies of nature.

A spirit is a harp attuned to respond to the touch of myriad forces. It is placed in the center of these multitudinous energies, coming in from every direction. It is sensitive to the touch of the sun, the moon and the planets, and to that of the farthest star that twinkles on the verge of the Milky Way; not in the sense of astrology, but in as faithful a manner. If the magnetic needle trembles because of a spot in the sun; if the magnetic currents of the earth are disturbed by activity of the solar disc, can we for a moment doubt but the more delicately ethereal spiritual perception will feel such disturbances? The sweet influence of the Pleiades has more than poetic meaning, and the cold light of the moon brings on its beams the breath of love.

It is well known that many diseases are aggravated by the approach of night, while others are most severe during the day. All nervous pains become intensified at the approach of night--a fact admitted, but referred by material science to the imagination, the fancy having free reign during the silent hours of darkness. During the day, the half of the earth illuminated is positive to the other unilluminated hemisphere. Hence the sensations of evening are different from those of morning. We have enjoyed the light and been positive during the day; when night advances, we become passive in the enveloping darkness, and enter a state twin sister to death, to arise in the morning again to meet the positive day.

Sleep during the night is more restoring than during the day--a distinction recognized by animals and plants. Night is no more terrible than day, yet the mind, oppressed by the negative condition then imposed on all things, peoples it with fancies. The hour of midnight is the established season for ghostly appearances. He who boldly walks along the churchyard path at noonday, would fain whistle to keep his courage up at the hour of midnight. Even Haeckel, the great naturalist, confesses that as the evening fell on him, while alone on the extreme point of Ceylon, and the shadows deepened on the weird forest and lonely sea, an "uncanny" feeling crept over him.

And the soul moves in the circle of the seasons; not only has human life its Spring, Summer, Autumn, and Winter; in the long three score years and ten, it swings through this circle with each succeeding procession of seasons, and experiences the changing impressions they so rapidly bring.

Unconscious Sensitiveness.

SILENCE AND RECEPTIVITY.--I sit down with the friend of my heart, and neither speak a word; we visit in close communion of souls, in silence; spoken words would be only jarring discord. The shallow mind is supplied with a wind of words: like a dictionary he is all words, but without a thought. The highest thought, the most profound feelings, are beyond the sphere of speech.

The restless wind is ever sighing; the restless, unbalanced soul is ever chattering its half-formed thoughts. The shallow brook splashes and dashes over its bed with noisy tongue; the deep river flows onward without a ripple on its broad surface to tell of its tremendous power.

If we would learn of nature we must retire to her solitudes and let no one intrude. The dearest and nearest may draw with well meaning hands an opaque vail between us and the sun. In the solitude of the forest, by the shores of the sullen sea, and in the depths of star-lit night, we rest as dwarfs, overpowered by the stupendous elements, yet the center of all forces and phenomena. We are in the vortex of creative energies, and if we silently question, the answers fall as soon as our minds are receptive to them. In its adoration of the boundless, the soul mirrors its own infinitude. The shoreless expanse of sea, with sky and wave blending, lost in mist, in the never-reached horizon; the depths of stars, beyond and beyond, in vistas leading out into absolute void, beyond all created things--to such the soul acknowledges kinship, and in them finds its satisfaction. The thoughts of the stars are untongued, but they vibrate across the limitless ether, and are eloquent to the receptive mind.

Immeasurably more needful of receptivity born of silence, is the contact with the infinite realm of spirit. The ocean of being, invisible, is before us. We may not dictate, nor with blatant cry make demands. We shall be grateful for a grain of manna from the heavenly skies; we may gather a full repast. As spiritual beings, into the warp and woof of whose existence enter the strands of immortal life, we are capable of comprehending the laws of this unseen, and heretofore unknown universe. As suns are pulsating centers of light, spiritual beings are pulsating centers of thought, and as light waves go out circling until lost on the remotest coast line of the universe, so thought-waves go out from the thinking mind, and are caught up by all minds receptive to them.

By the sea, the soul sees the inner world expressed by a series of changing pictures. The ships sailing from harbor, with all their white sails set, and bent to the breeze which wafts them into the gray mist until lost to view, express the voyage of human beings. The white birds, with flapping wings, are the purposeless spirits of the air. The stars, what consolation they have given the wretched in long ages of suffering, by their eternal placidity, their quietude from the feverish follies which we know intuitively belong to a lower life.

The truly receptive mind is least alone when alone. Then it becomes the headland against which beat the waves of thought from every thinking being in the universe. Like the telegraph receiver, it picks out the thoughts to which it is sensitive, and the others go on to those receptive to them. It thus becomes apparent that there can be an education superior to all others; the education of receptivity, or sensitiveness to the thought atmosphere or psychic-ether. Not that this can take the place of the ordinary training of the faculties, for their training, rudely performed as it is, often leads to a high sensitiveness; more often leads away from it. The poet is most sensitive to poetic thought, and in this sense is a medium, not only for individual poets, but, perhaps, unconsciously, for the inseparable thoughts of all. The truly great statesman receives influx from the United Congress of all past leaders. Through the sensitive preacher, all preachers of the past find tongue. The man of science, if successful in research, may be praised for skill and faithfulness, but beyond these qualities are the impressions descending from all who think or ever have thought on their special subjects. There is a sensitiveness of organization, and not of culture, which makes of the possessor a mouth-piece, an instrument, such as it is. There is a sensitiveness, better here called receptivity, which comes of right culture, and is the highest form of mediumship, though its possessor may be wholly unconscious of his gift.

RECEPTIVITY AND GREATNESS.--Here and there are those who by organization are sensitive and ready instruments to bless the world with the light of higher spheres. There have been many in the past fifty years. Centuries have gone by and not one of these barren--centuries during which man remained stationary or retrograded into dense ignorance.

As mountain peaks catch the light of morning when all the valleys and plains below are wrapped in darkness, so these sensitives arise into the atmosphere of spirit, and bathe their foreheads in its glory.

Who should be more sensitive to the urgencies of a threatened state than he who has the responsibilities of government? Whom would the departed statesman, who, loving his country, seek to impress, if not the ones in power, who could make such impressions available? But those in power may not be impressible, and this is most unfortunate for the state. They MAY be, and then it can be truthfully said that the forces of heaven fight its battles.

Such an one was Lincoln. His receptive mind responded to the thought waves of the psychic atmosphere, and he became the center of a thought-vortex--the concentration of unnumbered intelligences--with the holy spiritual fervor of the sage and prophet. Feeling himself called to a mighty task, and consecrated to its accomplishment, his great and earnest soul responded to the breath of inspiration. He was misunderstood by men because he acted from motives they could not comprehend, and which were uncomprehended by himself; but during the years of darkness, anxiety and care, the cabinet on which he relied was not the executive officers, but one formed of those Fathers of the Republic, who, on the hour of its birth, gave its flag to the breezes of heaven. He failed at times; disasters came, representing the periods when the clouds obscured the clear light of inspiration. He disregarded the impressions of impending danger, and disobedience sealed the record of his labors with his blood!

Then in invention, the contrivances by which the elements are harnessed and become willing servants, we take one man as an illustration. A poor uneducated country lad, with a simple knowledge of telegraphy sufficient to send messages over the wires, that is all--no college learning, no one to assist, to direct, to advise. He soon entered a field where no mortal could advise, where no mortal had been or knew aught to advise him. He became sensitive, and the secret chambers of the lightning were unlocked to him. What to other men who had devoted a life-time of study was obscure and mysterious, became to him the ABC to higher readings. He sent his voice across the continent, he recorded the sounds so that the instrument would in all after years give us back the tones of those we love; he prolonged the lightning's lurid flash into a continuous blaze, and converted night into day; he made the current leap from the wire to the passing train and over an intangible wire from ship to ship, across leagues of sea.

TRUE INSPIRATION.--OLE BULL.--What is meant by the oft-repeated assertion that great and exceptional persons are inspired? More especially in music and poetry is the influx from some foreign source distinctly marked. Ole Bull, the king of all violin players, was, by his own confession, subject to an influence beyond himself. When a boy, he was attempting, unaided, to translate into musical sounds the splendor of his ideal, a "voice" encouraged him constantly with "Bravo!" which he accepted as a sign that he was doing well. Unlike Socrates' "demon," instead of being always the same, it was that of many celebrated musicians. On one occasion, the voice of Handel murmured in his ear after a rendition of that composer's "Hallelujah Chorus," "Only shadow music sung by shadows." "My soul asked, 'Where, then, is the substance, Master?'" "In my world," the voice replied, "where alone all things are real, and music is the speech."

PAGANINI.--Of Paganini it was said that he not only enchanted his listeners, but played as one enchanted, losing consciousness, and throughout his performances remained as one entranced. So real were musical conceptions flashed on his mind, that they became objective, and danced before him in wild expression of rhythmic motion.

How far the ecstasy of all true musicians may account for their super-normal efforts, depends on the meaning accepted of ecstasy. It really is a state of sensitiveness to harmonious sounds, which at its best differs little from the most exalted form of clairvoyance, or, perhaps better, clair-audience.

BLIND TOM.--All have heard of Blind Tom, an idiotic negro, uncouth, untaught, yet who was able to play the most intricate music, in a manner only attainable to others by years of study and practice. His improvisations were the wonder and delight of the listeners, and were dashed off with the fingers of what might truly have been regarded as an automaton. By what method could his astonishing facility of execution, delicacy of expression, and masterly touch be explained? He was never taught a lesson in music, was incapable of forming a continuous train of thought; yet no conservatory ever graduated a superior performer. We are forced to accept one of two conclusions: either that he was of himself superior to any one in musical ability, or that he derived this gift from an outside source. The first, on the face of it, appears an absurdity. He was no more the cause of the music he produced than was the piano on which he played. Both were instruments, he standing between the force and its effect.

HANDEL.--In the sphere of sacred music, perhaps Handel stands without a peer. So far above the ordinary level is his sublime work, that he receives not his full mead of praise; for we applaud most that which echoes some part of ourselves, and with his strains we are bowed in humility and awe. In twenty-three days he produced "The Messiah," a work which, for vastness of conception and exquisite finish, is the grandest and most perfect choral work the world has ever known. He belonged to no school, has no imitators, for he is too far removed for imitation to be attempted. Well has it been said that the power of such souls baffles criticism. That they tower so far above the common level, and possess such exceptional mental and moral powers, leads to the supposition that they touch a thought-sphere not touched by those less sensitively endowed.

BEECHER.--This great preacher, who left Plymouth pulpit vacant, a vacancy which never can be filled, is a fine illustration of these views.

The man and his inspiration were constantly struggling for mastery. He would advance, on the tide of that inspiration, to the very brink of the precipice of heterodoxy; his large heart and enthusiasm carrying him and his hearers far beyond the limits of their narrow creeds, and then recovering himself he would recoil, restate, explain and hedge against the severity of the criticism provoked. But constantly he gained ground, and carried his hearers with him. He never retreated quite as far as he advanced, and in later years the inspiring power had educated the man to its level, and he bravely and boldly stood by his words. For an entire generation he stood in his pulpit, a divine oracle, every Sunday having an audience of the entire country, and as an elevating, educating power, was immeasurable. He broke the fetters from the slave; he broke the fetters of superstition from millions, more bondsmen than the negro slave. If you were to gather up all that he has written it would make a library of itself, and yet there is little of all that he has written or spoken that has permanent value, or will endure. Its value consisted not in its enduring qualities; rather in its being tentative; steps leading upward, and of no use after once being passed over. He did not, he could not, preach the ultimate truth. The laity, as a conservative force, restrained him. Like an eagle burdened with a great weight, he carried his church and the world forward, and with every new wave of inspiration the burden grew lighter, but he never was quite free.

The limitation of the individual always stands in the path of perfect inspiration. He was forced to speak after the forms of the creeds and beliefs which he inherited, and believed by those he would instruct. Those beliefs were perishing, and his modifications did not quite grasp the whole truth, and hence must disappear. But through him a mighty influence was exerted; not such as may be likened to the avalanche which plunges down the mountain, but like the breath of spring, melting the snow and ice of winter, warming the indurated soil, and making possible the bursting forth of flowers, the prophecies of autumn fruitage.

It is remarkable that few writers have given the world more than one master-piece, and often a single short poem, out of a mass of composition, is all that remains of permanent value. Gray's "Elegy" and "Sweet Home" are examples. The genius which could write these wonderful poems ought to have been able to write others equally perfect; yet only once did the authors touch the pure fount of inspiration. Mrs. Julia Ward Howe in such a moment wrote the "Battle Hymn of the Republic," which, unlike anything ever before written, and unlike anything else she ever wrote, became the marching song of a nation along the pathway of justice.

MRS. HARRIET BEECHER STOWE wrote before and after the production of "Uncle Tom's Cabin," works of some merit, but nothing that approached the wonderful story that did more to arouse the nation to the wrongs of slavery than all other influences combined. According to her own words, she composed in a state in which she was overwhelmed with the subject and forced to write as she did.

DICKENS entered the same state, and with such distinctness were his characters brought before him, that he heard their voices, and his dialogues were the work of a reporter rather than of a composer.

BUNYAN.--Perhaps no book ever exerted a greater influence than "Pilgrim's Progress," written by one who in his youth was wild and godless, a tramping tinker and rough soldier, uneducated and unversed in literary invention. He possessed in a prominent degree the sensitive temperament, as his portrait shows, and a fine mental endowment, however uncultivated it might have been. So long as Bunyan was a part of the jostling world, he was like other men. His sensitiveness could only be made valuable by isolation, and that came to him in an unlooked for manner by his incarceration in jail. There his spirit gained freedom. It became susceptible to the thoughts of another sphere, and he wrote that remarkable book, which has pleased and strengthened millions of struggling souls. Afterwards, when liberated, he became one of the fanatics among whom he was cast, and his writings and speech were of no value, except as they faintly echoed what he had written in his "Pilgrim." Once only had the conditions essential to sensitiveness been his, and then it was forced upon him, and the result was one book of value, and no more. The success of that book destroyed the conditions for the reception of anything as pure, bringing around him the jarring conflict of religious fanaticism.

TENNYSON.--The sensitive condition of Tennyson has been graphically described by himself, in words which leave no misunderstanding. In a letter written in 1874 to a friend, he says: "I have never had any revelation through anesthetics, but a kind of waking trance (this for want of a better term) I have frequently had, quite up from boyhood, when I have been all alone. This has often come upon me through repeating my own name to myself silently till, all at once, as it were, out of the intensity of the consciousness of the individuality, the individuality itself seemed to dissolve and fade away into boundless being; and this is not a composed state, but the clearest of the clearest, the surest of the surest, utterly beyond words, where Death was an almost laughable impossibility, the loss of personality, (if so it were) seeming no extinction, but the only true life. I am ashamed of my feeble description. Have I not said the state was utterly beyond words?"

Illustrations to an unlimited extent might be drawn from the lives of authors, artists, inventors, statesmen and warriors, in confirmation of the views expressed.

In fact, scarcely a single one of all the brilliant names that head the list on the scroll of fame but might be taken as an example.

THE GREAT LEADERS in history, statesmanship, war, literature, the arts, in science and in invention, few in number, appear like centers on whom the thoughts of their time converge, and from whom they are radiated. They are moved by forces beyond themselves, and plan wiser than they know. Napoleon schemed for his own aggrandizement, but above him was a power which directed his efforts. The art of war was an open book to him, and his tactics, the fresh product of his teeming brain, were a constant surprise and menace to his enemies. Until his mission was accomplished he was invincible. When he transcended that, which was to break down the absurd distinctions of feudalism, and make the serf a man, and in arrogant pride looked on the nations as his prey, the conditions of his receptivity were destroyed and his defeat assured.

These great minds have no ancestral lineage, they rarely transmit their talent to their offspring. For a brief moment, that of their great achievement, they gain the heights never before reached, and not again to be reached by their posterity.

CONCENTRATION.--It has been said that great concentration of mind--the ability to exclude all objects and subjects except the one under consideration--is the prime factor of genius, and an adequate explanation of its achievements. In other words, concentration is another name for sensitiveness. What is concentration? Is it not a mental state in which one idea, a group of ideas, dominate; and where is the difference between this state and the hypnotic? Is it not a condition of exceeding sensitiveness to ideas related to the dominating? There really is slight distinguishing difference between the concentration of writer, speaker, or inventor, and the mesmeric, or hypnotic state of the sensitive. All the difference observable is from the side on which the subject is approached.

This concentration has been called attention to by some authors, who would make genius itself dependent entirely on attention, which Buffon speaks of as protracted patience. The mind that can take hold of the thread of a subject, and hold fast to it in all its intricacies to the end, is enabled to do so by superior attention. Concentration is more expressive, and under whatever name, the same mental state is designated. The profound student always falls into it when absorbed in his work, and becomes "absent-minded," which is an expression commonly used to explain one of the most inexplicable mental states. When under control of the will, such concentration of mental power becomes priceless to its possessor. It is similar to the hypnotic state, with none of its disadvantages, and removed to a higher plane. The mind in this highly sensitive condition is impressible to the thought waves in the psychic-ether. On the other hand, when this concentration or attention is not controllable by the will, the condition of the unfortunate individual is most deplorable. He is lost in reverie, a dreamy, misty state of mind which unfits him for the duties of practical life. The difference is that between forgetfulness of duty, which has been the butt of endless ridicule by the world and of burlesque on the stage, and the reaches of thought attained by the philosopher, and the divine songs of the poet. The first essential requisite of profound thought is abstraction from the distractions of all matters except the one in hand. Ability to thus concentrate the mind at pleasure may be inherited or the product of education. In fact, correct education may be said to consist mainly in the control of the attention, and the ability to concentrate the mind on the one subject presented.

The higher education of the future will recognize and give prominence to the cultivation of this hitherto ignored faculty.

It is one of the possibilities of the future to encourage the culture of the sensitive faculty, and the results will be far more wonderful in normal education than now arises from what seems abnormal, and the product of chance.

Sensitiveness, as has been shown in the preceding pages, is possessed by all in greater or less degree, and may be cultivated like any other mental quality. As its laws and conditions are more thoroughly understood and its inestimable value realized, it will become a part of all substantial educational training.

THE EXTENSION OF THIS THEORY INTO THE LIFE BEYOND.--This theory, without calling to its aid spiritual beings, marks out the laws by which such beings may control the sensitive and become cognizant of the thoughts of each other. Man being a spirit, limited by a physical body, through the sensitive state, under certain conditions, he breaks away from his limitations and feels the waves of thought created by others through the psychic-ether.

When freed from the physical body the spirit must possess the same power in larger degree and impress its thoughts on the sensitive in the same manner. Sensitive beyond mortal conception in its most exalted state, it is in connection with all spiritual intelligences, and a converging and diverging center of telegraphic communication. As it advances in this sensitiveness, distance becomes a less and less factor, until eliminated, and a thought sent forth wings its way until it meets the one for whom it was intended.

Thus, what has been made the toy of a leisure hour, the imperfect attempts at thought-reading, mesmeric control of the will, and the mystery of communion of minds sympathetic, are really the crude manifestations of an undeveloped faculty, which, after the evolution wrought by death, becomes the glory of spirit-existence.

Prayer in the Light of Sensitiveness and Thought Waves.

When President Garfield was lying tortured by the wound which caused his death, the prayers of a whole nation arose as one united voice for his recovery. From sixty thousand pulpits petitions to the throne of grace ascended. There were days set apart for united appeal to God. He was eminent in the church as in war and politics, and if prayer ever received answer, it would seem that it should be in his case. Yet the good man, the scholar, the statesman and theologian died, just as he would have died had no petition been sent to the throne of grace. The ocean ship, freighted with passengers, is broken through by an iceberg, and slowly filling, settles down into the waves. Wildly the best and purest men and women pray to God for help, but the ship is not thereby sustained, or delayed a single moment in her final plunge into the abysses of the sea.

On occasions of great public calamity, where drought blasts the harvest, locusts devour the fields, or pestilence rages, days are set apart for prayer. Every minister of the gospel and every layman daily prays with utmost fervor. Yet the rain falls not, the locusts devour, and the pestilence pursues its way without shadow of turning. Prayer in such cases is as hopeless as it would be if the maker should stand on a railroad track, and, when he saw a train approaching, pray to God to stop it. It is a petition for the impossible.

In one way it yields results, often of an astonishing character. If the makers are sincere, the attitude of prayer harmonizes and strengthens their faculties, and enables them to bear with greater fortitude the vicissitudes of time; to bear, but not avert, impending fate. How many captives chained in dungeons have, in imitation of the apostle, prayed fervently with perfect faith that their chains might fall off, and the bars of their prison door be drawn aside, and met with no response. How many zealous martyrs have been led to the stake, praying to Jesus for deliverance which came not; and Jesus himself, in the hour of his mortal agony, prayed to the Father, to be answered by silence, and to find bitterness and mockery; a cross and a crown of thorns, where he had expected a throne and the glittering scepter of the nations.

The once all-powerful belief in the ability of delegated men to control events and elements by supplication to the Deity, which made the "medicine men," the priests and jugglers, the tyrants of mankind, has now, in civilized countries, dwindled into the intercessions for moral help, and an occasional prayer for physical changes, as for rain in times of drought, the staying of grasshoppers, or the approach of disease.

It is difficult for the gospel minister to give up entirely the role of the "medicine man," and cease to pray for the sick in the misty hope that God will answer. It is almost as troublesome for the preacher to let go his hold on the weather, and not follow the Indian's rattling gourd, shaken at the sky, with prayer for the same object.

This is the degradation of prayer, and the preacher clasps hands with the juggler. That this pretense is yet maintained, is made most remarkably apparent in a work on prayer recently published. An incident in the life of President Finney, of Oberlin College, copied from its pages, will amply suffice to illustrate this anachronism, a belief of savage man forced into the highest civilized thought.

There was drought in Oberlin, and the thin, hard clay soil of that region suffered severely from a total failure for three months, of rain. Clouds promised the desired moisture, but hovered over the lake, and poured out their waters there. This they did day after day, raising the hopes of the anxious, and then drifting away.

Finney, who was an enthusiast, was walking in the street one day, when a friend met him and said: "I should like to know what you mean by preaching that God is always wise and always good, when you see him pouring out that great rain on the lake, where it can do no good, and leaving us to suffer so terribly for want of the wasted water?"

Finney said: "His words cut me to the very heart; I turned and ran home to my closet, fell on my knees, and told the Lord what had been said to me, and besought him, for the honor of his great name, to confound this caviler, and show forth the glory of his power, and the greatness of his love. I pleaded with him that he had encouraged his people to pray for rain, and now the time had come for him to show his power, and his faithfulness as a hearer of prayer. Before I rose from my knees there was a sound of a rushing mighty wind. I looked out, and lo, the heavens were black; clouds were rolling up, and rain soon fell in torrents, continuing for two full hours."

Those who are acquainted with the lake region know the peculiarity of these storms, and will readily understand the rapidity of their coming. They require no prayer to move them, and that the coincidence of the rain and the prayer should be endorsed by leaders in theology, is a strange instance of mental aberration, or, as Darwin would say, atavism. The absurdity of the representation apparently escapes the notice of those who accept it. The zealous Finney telling an Omnipotent God what he ought to do to show his power and keep his promise for his own interest and reputation, as though the rain was not withheld for some good purpose well known by the Omnipotent! And then by his pleading, this little President of a then obscure college, changed the will and purpose of the Almighty, and brought the rain to a narrow section of country, leaving regions beyond equally suffering without a drop of moisture!

Such instances prove too much. They maintain the changefulness of God, and the power of man to persuade Him to alter the course of the elements. Mr. Finney heralds with ostentatious pride this case when the clouds came at his call; he does not tell us of the prayers he and all the praying people of that region had daily offered for weeks and months for the same object, which brought no moisture!

Rain is sure to come at some time, and if the seasons of prayer be continued long enough, the last one will surely be followed by rain.

This instance is introduced to illustrate the limitation of the power of prayer. The insensible elements can not be influenced. The clouds and the winds, the storm and the earthquake, will not come or go at our bidding, or the invocation, even, of a saint.

Yet earnest prayer, within fixed limitations, may be and has been answered, as is proven by innumerable witnesses. Not by a personal God to whom the appeal is made, but by harmonizing the prayer-giver with subtile spiritual forces, which work in ways not comprehended by a gross view of the world. When we consider human and spiritual beings as laved by an ocean of attenuated substance, elastic and receptive beyond comprehension, and that each being is a vortex of vibrations, we understand how from an intensely wrought mind vibrant thoughts go forth, and although they strike an infinite number of individuals who are not sensitive to them, they find others in mortal bodies or spiritual, as harps like attuned set each other in vibration, and move those thus receptive to answer their appeals. The power and strength given by prayer arise from this harmonizing of their being by spiritual aspiration, which lift the mind into the realm of superior spiritual forces. It is then that the appeal to God goes forth in vibrations, to be recognized by spirit friends, and by them conveyed to mortals who have the ability to respond, or directly reach some responsive mind in the mortal body.

The following narrative of Dr. Joseph Smith, of Warrington, England, which is accredited by the journal of the Society for Psychological Research, May, 1885, is a fine illustration of what is popularly known as God's answer to prayer:

"I was sitting one evening reading when a voice came to me, saying:

"'Send a loaf to James Grady's.' I continued reading, and the voice continued with greater emphasis, and this time it was accompanied with an irresistible impulse to get up. I obeyed, and went into the village and bought a loaf of bread, and seeing a lad at the shop door, I asked him if he knew James Grady. He said he did, so I had him carry it, and say that a gentleman sent it. Mrs. Grady was a member of my class, and I went down next morning to see what came of it, when she told me that a strange thing had happened to her last night. She said she wished to put the children to bed, but they began to cry for want of food, and she had nothing to give them. She then went to prayer, to ask God to give them something, soon after which the lad came to the door with the loaf. I calculated on inquiry that the prayer and the voice I heard exactly coincided in point of time."

As a member of his class, a close connection existed between Dr. Smith and Mrs. Grady, and he was thereby receptive to the eager appeal she made, incited by her children's cry for bread.

The case of Henry Young Stilling has become a text in most orthodox books on the subject of prayer. He was a physician at the court of the Grand Duke of Baden, the intimate friend of Goethe, who, impressed with his remarkable experiences, urged him to write an account of his life.

Stilling desired to study medicine at a university, and in an answer to prayer to know which he should choose was directed to Strasburg. In order to attend that school he required a thousand dollars, and he had only forty-six; yet with this he started on his journey, freely relying on heavenly aid. On reaching Frankfort, he had only a dollar left. He made his case known by prayer. Walking on the street he met a merchant, who, learning his purpose of attending the university, asked where the money was to come from. Stilling replied that he had only one dollar, but his Heavenly Father was rich and would provide for him. "Well, I am one of your Father's stewards," said the merchant, and handed him thirty-three dollars. Settled at Strasburg, his fee to the lectures became due and must be paid by Thursday evening, or his name stricken from the roll. He spent the day in prayer, and at five o'clock nothing had come. His anxiety became unbearable, when a knock was heard at his door, and his landlord entered and inquired how he liked the room, and if he had money. "No, I have no money," cried Stilling in despair. "I see how it is," replied the landlord; "God has sent me to help you," and handed him forty dollars. Stilling threw himself on the floor and thanked God, while the tears rained from his eyes. His whole life's experience was of a like character. He prayed constantly to God, and at the last moment his necessities were supplied.

How difficult it is to suppose that God interested himself especially in one of thousands of students, overlooking the others, equally poor and needy, and as earnest in their efforts! How easy to suppose that an angel friend, foreseeing the great capabilities of Stilling, interested himself, and by influencing this or that mind smoothed the way, and furnished the means he imperatively needed. It will be remarked that at no time were his necessities exceeded. No one gave him lavishly, or more than sufficed for his urgent needs.

Rev. H. Bushnell, in his "Nature and the Supernatural," refers to an interesting incident he learned on his visit to California. The man had hired his little house of one room, in a new trading town that was planted last year, agreeing to give a rent of ten dollars a month. When the pay day came he had nothing to meet the demand, nor could he see whence the money was to come. Consulting with his wife, they agreed that prayer, so often tried, was their only hope. They went according to prayer, and found assurance that their want would be supplied.

When the morning came the money did not. The rent owner made his appearance earlier than usual. As he entered the door their hearts began to sink, whispering that now, for once, their prayer had failed. But before the demand was made, a neighbor came and called out the untimely visitor, engaging him in conversation a few minutes at the door. Meanwhile, a stranger came in saying, "Doctor, I owe you ten dollars for attending me in a fever, and here is the money." He could not remember either the man or the service, but was willing to be convinced, and had the money when the rent owner again entered. The same explanation applies here as to the preceding.

The following indicates not an answer to the prayer, but a direct communication. It is related by Dr. Wilson, of Philadelphia: "The packet ship, 'Albion,' full of passengers from America, was wrecked on the coast of Ireland, and the news was that all on board had perished. A minister near Philadelphia, reading a list of the lost, found the name of one of the members of his congregation, and went immediately to inform the wife of the sad fact. She had been earnestly praying during the voyage of her husband, and had received assurance of his safety amid great danger. Hence, to the astonishment of her pastor, after he had informed her of the shipwreck, and showed her the list of names of those who were lost, she told him that it was a mistake, that her husband had been in extreme peril, but was not dead. When the next tidings were received it proved that her husband was among the passengers, and had been in great peril, but that he had escaped, and was the only one saved."

There could be no connection between the wife's prayer and safety of her husband, but the state of mind induced by prayer allowed her to receive the message of his safety.

The celebrated artist, Washington Allston, refined and sensitive to a fault, had at first to struggle with great difficulties, and endure the pinchings of poverty. At one time he was reduced to the want of even a loaf of bread for himself and wife. In despair he locked himself in his studio and earnestly prayed for assistance. While thus engaged, there was a knock at the door, and opening it a stranger appeared, who inquired if the artist still possessed the beautiful painting, "The Angel Uriel." Mr. Allston drew it from a corner, and brushed off the dust. The stranger said he had greatly admired it when it was on exhibition, and inquired the price. The artist replied that as no one seemed to appreciate it he had ceased to offer it. "Will four hundred pounds purchase?" said the stranger. "I never dared ask one-half of that." "Then it is mine," exclaimed the visitor, who explained that he was the Marquis of Stafford, leaving the artist overwhelmed with gratitude.

Where the answer to prayer follows so directly the appeal, we may suppose that the intensity of thought may affect directly the individual who responds. Thus, when Allston was so despairing, his thoughts would go widely forth, and the Marquis of Stafford having seen the painting, and desiring it, might have the thought of it awakened, and be thereby drawn at the special time to the artist's studio. Of course the case is also open to the direct intervention of angelic messengers, for all this class of facts intimately blend, and are controlled by the same general laws, and it is difficult to determine to which of the two causes they should be referred. The door that admits angelic beings makes the influence of thought waves also possible.

The cure of Melancthon by the prayers of Luther is well known to the student of the Reformation. The former had been given over to die, when Luther rushed to the death-bed of his loved friend with tears and exclamations of agony. Melancthon was aroused and said: "O Luther, is this you? Why do you not let me depart in peace?" "We can't spare you yet, Philip," was Luther's answer. Then he bowed down for a long hour in prayer, until he felt he had been answered. Then he took Melancthon's hand, who said: "Dear Luther, why do you not let me depart in peace?" "No, no, Philip, we can not spare you from the field of labor;" and added, "Philip, take this soup, or I will excommunicate you." Melancthon took the soup, began to revive, and lived many years to assist the sturdy reformer with his facile pen. Luther went home and told his wife, in joyous triumph, that "God gave me my brother, Melancthon, in direct answer to prayer."

Now, such a cure would be called faith cure, or magnetic healing. The state of feeling induced by long and fervent prayer was the source of magnetic power, and therein, and not through the direct intervention of God, was the prayer answered.

Bishop Bowman gives the following account of the unexpected recovery of Bishop Simpson, when he was supposed to be dying:

"I remember once, when there was a conference at Mount Vernon, Ohio, at which I was present, Bishop James was presiding one afternoon, and after reading a despatch saying that Bishop Simpson was dying in Pittsburg, asked that the conference unite in prayer, that his life might be saved. We knelt, and Taylor, the great street preacher, led. After the first few sentences, in which I joined with my whole heart, my mind seemed to be at ease, and I did not pay much attention to the rest of the prayer only to notice its beauty. When we arose from our knees, I turned to a brother and said, 'Bishop Simpson will not die; I feel it.' He assured me that he had received the same impression. The word was passed around, and over thirty ministers present said they had the same feelings. I took my book and made a note of the hour and circumstance. Several months afterwards, I met Bishop Simpson, and asked him what he did to recover his health. He did not know; but the physician had said it was a miracle. He said, that one afternoon, when at the point of death, the doctor left him, saying that he should be left alone (by the doctor) for half an hour. At the end of that time, the doctor returned, and noticed a great change. He was startled, and asked the family what had been done, and they replied, nothing at all. That half hour, I find, by making allowance for difference of localities, was just the time we were praying for him at Mount Vernon. From that time on he steadily improved, and has lived to bless the Church and humanity."

Bishop Bowman adds:

"On the God who has so often answered my prayers, I will still rely, scientific men and philosophers to the contrary notwithstanding." The "scientific man" would reply that he had no desire to dispute the fact as stated, but, instead of a personal God who had struck down Bishop Simpson with disease, changing his purpose because supplicated by the ministerial conference, the intense fervency of thought of that conference united in prayer had gone forth in a magnetic beam, and given the suffering patient the strength of a new life. If there was divine agency, it stood back of the laws of spiritual forces, in which case, prayer was only a means of preparation, unitizing, harmonizing and directing.

He was affected just the same as he would have been had he been in the conference hall, for distance, as has been repeatedly shown, is an unimportant element in the exercise of these psychic forces.

There are several charitable institutions which their founders claim to have been entirely supported by means of donations made in answer to prayer. As these are often brought forward in evidence of the direct answer to prayer, they become of interest to the student of this subject.

The Bristol Orphan Home is typical of its class. George Muller, its founder, began with no wealth, aside from his sublime faith in his appeals for divine aid. In his Thirty-sixth Annual Report, he says that in 1875 his faith was put to trial most severely. He commenced the year with $20,000 in his treasury, which in three months was reduced one-half, or only enough to meet expenses for a single month. The treasury had never been as low, and the number of orphans had doubled. He fervently prayed, as the situation became more alarming, and at the end of the month so many donations flowed in he had $48,000.

In the forty-one years this institution has been conducted, during which no appeal for charity has been made directly, except through prayer, $3,325,000 has been received. As the results of its use, 46,400 persons have been taught in schools wholly sustained, and tens of thousands in schools assisted; 96,000 Bibles, 247,000 Testaments, and 180,000 smaller portions of the Scriptures circulated; above 53,500,000 tracts and books in various languages distributed; of late years 170 missionaries annually assisted; 4,677 orphans cared for; five large edifices built, at a cost or $575,000, able to accommodate 2,050 orphans.

Such an institution may have no organized soliciting board on the earthly side, but of necessity must have on the spiritual side. It is a potent center of attraction to those who have means, and are looking about for some worthy object. The leaders, with self-abnegation, devote their lives to the unselfish work, and the angel messengers, with equal devotion, act as solicitors to those they are able to approach.

We may also regard as a potent factor, earnest prayer going out on waves of thought, and directly affecting susceptible minds, calling their attention to the great charity, and influencing them to sustain it.

This explanation of the effect of prayer, and of the causes contributing to its answering, while removing it from the realm of miracle, makes the subject one of absorbing interest. The Divine Spirit never directly answers, but there are laws and conditions through which the earnest spirit is granted the assistance it desires. It is a mistake to refer the answer directly to God, as it would be to say he supports the world in space by his extended arm. The Protestant churches hold as sacrilege the appeal to any being but God. The Catholics are more wise, and offer their prayers to their patron saints, by which comforting love and assuring affection are awakened by direct contact.

Christian Science, Mind Cure, Faith Cure--their Psychic Relations.

Out of the recently received views of spirit, derived by psychic investigations, have grown a number of systems, drawing nice distinctions between their claims, and, in some instances, expanding to the estate of psychic science, attempting not only to correlate the facts of spirit, but to found on them a system of morals. It is because of this that Christian science, theology, mind cure, faith cure, metaphysics, etc., have a place in the discussions entertained in this volume. Nearly all of these begin as methods of healing. Their first office is to restore health. Such has been the application of almost all new discoveries, which reveal and are half shrouded in mystery. Electricity and magnetism met this fate, and mesmerism was at first thought to be a curative agent for all diseases.

It is a singular fact that all religious systems, from that of the lowest savage, whose god is represented by a stick or a tuft of feathers, to the purest form of Christianity, depend on miraculous healing for their evidence of genuineness. It is true the weight of such evidence is constantly lessened with the advance of culture, yet it still remains in force, and by many believers is received as conclusive and final.

Charlatanism seized mesmerism, as it has everything new, and brought its healing potencies into disgrace by its ignorance and pretensions. The germ of truth was then, and from time to time has reappeared under startling names, and in some instances so changed as to appear superficially, as something entirely new. Those who scorn mesmerism received the new claimants, the only change being in name.

I propose to briefly examine some of these, and, if possible, find the rock of truth on which they rest.

CHRISTIAN SCIENCE.--First, as having attracted most attention, is Christian Science. It claims to be a system for curing the sick, preserving health, and a perfect moral guide in the conduct of life.

Healing the sick is only an accidental means of testing the genuineness of the devotee's belief. Healing is the first step on the lowest plane. It makes the proud claim of being the Science of Spirit, and as spirit is causation, Christian Science is the Science of Sciences. It aims to be a complete system of religion and morality, and demands the highest, most unselfish, devoted lives. It demands universal love, unfaltering charity; neither to think or act evil; the suppression of scorn and hate; a belief that all is good, for all is God, who is absolutely good.

It widely differs from the "faith cure," and mind cure, as it introduces and demands the highest excellence in the conduct of life, while the faith cure calls for simple faith in the means employed, or in the power of God.

Christian Science shows the source of its inspiration when it declares healing to be a test of faith and character.

THEOSOPHY resembles Christian Science, extending over the broadest field of morality, intellectuality, and spirit, eschewing healing as a test. The teachings of both, by appropriating all that is valuable in other doctrines, are similar. Theosophy, however, states one fundamental doctrine on which its superstructure rests. This is the pre-existence of the soul or spirit, and its repeated incarnations on earth. As this doctrine has been criticised elsewhere, the arguments against it need not be here introduced. As guides in the conduct of life they have nothing true which they can claim as new, and their distinctive features remain to be demonstrated, or are revived speculations and dreams of the world's dawn, when nature was a riddle and life a mystery.

THE FAITH CURE rests on the declarations of the Bible, that faith will remove mountains, and redeem the lost. When Christ or his disciples laid hands on the sick to heal, the first and paramount question was: Have they faith? There is curative power in faith. It is half gained to have the sick confident that they will recover; and the belief that they will be sustained by certain means often has more influence than the means.

THE MENTAL CURE asserts the superiority of the mind over the body, as a scientific fact, without appeal to God or faith. In vital essence, in making the body the servant of the mind, all these systems are identical. Christian Metaphysics and Christian Science, a difference of name, and mental cure, mind cure, etc., have the same basis. Each has enclosed a narrow field, and writes its name over the entrance. Christian Science, by making the greatest display, has become most conspicuous. Many of its propositions call forth no dissent, others are on their face too absurd to require contradiction.

The same line of argument will apply to all these systems, and they need not be taken separately.

INFLUENCE OF THE MIND OVER THE BODY.--The mind has a very great influence over the body, as has been remarked by those who have investigated the subject since the time of Hippocrates. The strongest mind sometimes is found in a weak body.

Lord Brougham, with a frail physique, performed the most Herculean mental tasks. It is said that he once worked one hundred and forty-four hours, or six consecutive days, and then slept all Saturday night, Sunday, and Sunday night, and was waked Monday morning by his valet to resume his labors.

The power of mind over the body is illustrated by the annals of explorers in the frigid zone, and in the deadly regions of the tropics. The leaders of such expeditions, with all the burden and responsibilities of their position, bear up better than their men, and rarely succumb to adversities to which the latter yield. The hardships met by Dr. Kane and Lieut. Greely are fresh in the mind; and the invincible Stanley, braving the savage foes and deadly malaria of the Black Continent, is another example. Such leaders, encouraged by the honors success will yield, and dreading the shame of defeat more than death, persevere against all opposing forces, while their men, with less at stake either to win or lose, sink, apathetically, before reaching the goal. In such cases, the will sustains the body, and shows its independence of the material forces which affect it.

In no instance is the control of mind over the sensations, affecting it through the body, shown with greater force than in the terrible ordeals of martyrdom. The weak and delicate woman, as well as the strong man, was bound on the rack, or subjected to the unspeakable horrors of the thumbscrew, burning pincers, or the smouldering fagots, and yet so far from uttering moans or sighs, smiled on their tormentors, or sang hozannas amid the flames. Their minds had risen to such exaltation that physical pain was unfelt, in fact, was a relief to the mental tension.

There is no pathological phenomena more freely attested than the sudden vitiation of the secretions by intense mental disturbances. A mother subjected to intense fright, or fear, will have her milk become poisonous to her babe. Dr. A. Combe mentions an instance where a mother left her child to assist the father in combat with a drunken soldier. After the fight was over she nursed the babe, which was strong and healthy. After a few minutes it ceased nursing, and sank dead in its mother's arms. The milk had become a virulent poison.

A lady with a violent temper was warned by her physician against indulging it while nursing her babe, and she had obeyed until the child was several months old, strong and healthy. At that time she became enraged at some trivial circumstance, and soon afterwards she nursed her babe, which became ill, and within an hour was dead. The changes wrought in the saliva by anger are well known. The bite of an enraged man is as much to be dreaded as that of a mad dog. Blood poisoning is almost a sure consequence of inoculation with the saliva of an angry man or brute.

Hydrophobia itself is probably a spontaneous production in canines subjected to starvation and ill-usage.

Great joy or grief produces secretions in the blood, which make it poisonous. The prostration by grief is only equaled by that of violent disease. The blood and all secretions therefrom become so affected that a long time is required to eliminate the morbific matter from the system. If this is not accomplished, lingering illness or death is the final result. This is distinct from sudden death, on the disclosure of some startling news, of grief or joy. The heart in these instances suddenly fails at the nervous shock. Successful labor is always invigorating, while unsuccessful is depressing. It was observed in the early mining days of California that a stranger passing the claims could readily discover those that paid and those that did not, by the manners of the men who were working them. If unsuccessful, they were depressed, ill with fevers and idle. If successful they were at work early and late, cheerful, well, and energetic.

Every pursuit that ennobles and elevates the mind, tranquilizes the system, enhances the general health, and prolongs life.

Such is the wonderful sway the mind holds over the body. On the other hand, we find the body exciting a powerful influence on the mind; so intense and complete that leading physiologists believe that the latter is a result of, and entirely dependent on, the former, and having no existence independent thereof.

The microscope has poured a flood of light on disease. In most cases, as with these epidemics and contagions, a specific germ is introduced into the blood and multiplies, feeding on the vital fluid. If taken into the system of a saint it will, by multiplication, produce the disease, just as certainly as in the system of the vilest malefactor. There would be more reasonable grounds for hoping to drive a hungry tiger away by mind cure, than the myriads of microbes that swarm in a drop of the fever patient's blood, or the microbes in the lungs of a consumptive.

Then is the system of mental cure a sham? No! It claims too much. When millions of bacilli swarm in the lungs, or the micrococcus brings on fever, shall we say we are well, that the mind, as a part of God, can not be sick, and as the body is fathered by the mind it can not be? We may say this, but the inexorable logic of facts refute our opinions. We might as well attempt to stay the spring of the tiger by an effort of will.

But there is a consideration back of this. By the accumulation of an endless series of taints of body and of mind, by false ideas and views of life, the power of mind over the body can not be compared with what it would be in a perfect state of right living. This is a consideration of greatest value, for it shows us, not what the past has been, but what the future may be.

The limits of the power of the mind over the body are not known, but with knowledge it ever enlarges its boundaries. The class of diseases which may be regarded as essentially corporal, as the previously mentioned contagions produced by microbes, the effects of ptomaines, and the mineral and vegetable poisons, has its limits contracted by mental influences. Individuals in the most terrible contagions, although in contact with the sick and dying, physicians, nurses or companions, are often exempt. Their systems do not furnish the necessary conditions for growth of the disease germs. Such individuals are fearless; and it is said that their indifference to danger is their shield of protection; yet it is often the case that when they become exhausted by excessive care, they fall victims. This conclusion, however, may be safely drawn, that there are conditions of body or mind, or of both, invulnerable to disease. What these conditions are we may not now know, but it is possible to know.

In these cases of purely physical disease, the body reacts on the mind, and the giving way of the will is the first indication of the approach of the malady. It is folly to talk of the will overcoming a disease that has insidiously sapped its foundation. This is not saying that were the wrong conditions of living righted, and the taints of heredity eliminated, the power of the will would not be able to maintain the body against all succeeding influences. But to reach that perfect state will require many generations of rightly directed culture.

If grief, anger, or excessive joy are able to vitiate secretions, and cause sickness and death, a happy frame of mind, intellectual exertion and moral excellence tend to the perfect health of these secretions. Health is a condition to be gained and kept by careful observance of its laws, and these laws are of the physical as well as mental being.

Whatever truth there is in these newly named theories of healing, is identically the same as that claimed by the mesmerists and magnetists. The process, the cause and effect, are the same under the name of Christian Science as that of mesmerism. In the large class of diseases called nervous, the soothing influence of another mind is of unmeasured benefit. Even the hope aroused that some mind is exciting its will to relieve, is beneficial. The strengthened will and imagination are wonderfully healing agencies. While the influence of the mind over the body is admitted without contradiction so long as the former is connected with the latter, the limitations of the physical world must be felt. There is a sickness of the mind, and of the body, and over the latter the mind has not full control. Yet with a race freed from hereditary taint, having for generations obeyed the laws of health until its conditions are fixed by heredity, it may not be said what the power of the mind may be.

If the mother can stamp her unborn child with the monstrosity she fancies in her fright; if she can impart the insane thirst for stimulants and the fiendish hate and cruelty of savages, might she not by glorified conditions, exalted motives, and the over-shadowing consciousness that her mind is divine, the creator of an immortal being, endow the child with angelic qualities and make it a divine being? The children of many generations of such mothers, what exalted spiritual and intellectual attainment would be their inheritance!

Nor should the mother alone be held responsible, as has been the custom. Divine motherhood is linked with divine fatherhood, the opposite element, but of equal value. The germinal impulse carries with it all that has entered into the lives of remotest parental ancestors, and the recipient mother acts upon it, and is reacted on, until her entire being, physical and spiritual, is modified. However grand the ideal excellence of the future, it is not realized in the present, and may not be for ages to come. The present race of men are born with the sins of all the past stamped into their constitutions. It is folly to teach that there is no sickness except in the mind; idle to teach faith can cure disease, the seeds of which were planted unnumbered generations ago, and grown rankly from parent to child. Purity, true nobility of life, spiritual culture, devotion to right, and obedience to the laws of health may be accepted and the ideal attempted, but not fully realized now.

Meanwhile, old methods must not be wholly discarded. Old remedies can not be safely cast aside. The lame must have their staff and crutch until strong enough to walk alone.

CONCLUSION.--The Ideal may be sketched in our fond fancy, and the attempt to realize it began by living a higher, nobler, purer life. Know we what this means? It means more than simple living. There is everything beyond that. What this means will be best comprehended by referring to the preceding pages, where it is taught that there is a thought-atmosphere, from which sensitive minds receive a glorious flood of inspiration. Magnetism, Mesmerism, Hypnotism, or the states of healing by Faith or Christian Science are but the temporary approaches to that one condition of sensitiveness. In that condition great changes may be affected in the vital forces promotive of the normal functions of the various organs, as fear, grief, remorse, etc., may disturb their healthy action, and induce pathological changes in them.

Death will come to all physical forms sooner or later, for it is as necessary to the fulfillment of our destiny as to the transformation of the caterpillar to the butterfly; but disease and all the sufferings, losses, and disappointments in its train, may be, and will be, eliminated, when mortal life is so ordered that it will constantly walk in the shadow of spiritual forces.

Then sickness will be regarded as a mark of ignorance, if not a crime.

What the Immortal State Must Be.

THE LEAD OF THE ARGUMENT.--In pursuing the study of the subjects presented in the preceding pages, the student often catches a glimpse of an intelligent force existing after the death of the physical being. This came through the facts presented by hypnotism, somnambulism, trance, clairvoyance, thought-transference, dreams, and the appearance of the deceased to near friends at a distance, at the time of, or soon after, the hour of dissolution.

The continuance of existence beyond the grave has been made to depend on belief in certain dogmas, or at least the condition of that life has been made thus dependent by the religious systems of the world. Now that science encroaches on the realm of faith, and these dogmas are questioned, and immortality which seemingly rests on and is supported by them, becomes doubtful; yet, if it be a fact that man has a spirit, which is immortal, this is the most over-shadowing fact in the universe; one of profoundest interest and most consonant with the desires of the human heart. Around it gather our fondest hopes and brightest dreams; by it the seeming disparity and injustice of this life are compensated; the tearful eye is dried; the broken heart finds balm, and the burdens of time and place cast aside, and the possibilities of the aspiring spirit may be realized. It is an unfailing staff in the hands of those who mourn the loved and lost, offering the only adequate consolation in the cruel hour when we stand by the couch of death, feeling that, beyond, darkness gathers thick and broods over a sea of eternal silence, from which only echo responds to our call of the name of the departed. Then it is that hope lifts our hearts from despair, and a positive assurance of the continuity of life is worth all else in the world.

THE BELIEF IN IMMORTALITY HAS BEEN MADE A CURSE.--This belief, so full of delight and rainbowed with anticipations, has been made, from the dawn of man's religious nature, the means of inflicting unspeakable tortures, both of mind and body. Selfishness thrust the priest between man and the invisible world of spirit, and made immortality the instrument wherewith it could rule with diabolical despotism over mankind. Even when the rain-maker shook his rattling calabash at the sky, and beseeched the moisture-giving clouds to send down rain, the priestly order had fast hold on the superstitious savage; and in all the transformations of history, surging with the coming and going of countless generations and the ebb and flow of empires, never for a moment has this grip been loosened. The power of the temporal ruler has been second to that of the class who held the keys of life beyond the grave. What if the king could cast into a dungeon, condemn to the cross or the flames? That were pain for a moment, or, at most, for the few years of this life; and of what insignificance these short years, or the most terrible tortures human ingenuity could invent, to the infinite tortures extending through an eternal existence? Pharaoh might command Egypt to-day, but, to-night, his spirit would be summoned before the tribunal of the Dead; and those austere priestly judges would decide whether he be cast to the crocodiles of the Nile to become extinct, or again, clad in his mummified body, resurrected and purified, a companion of the gods.

What a position for an ignorant man! Immortality is the Promethean curse, enabling the vultures to inflict never-ending torments. The sweetest boon is oblivion, and that is denied. The sun may fade from the heavens and the stars cease to shine; but the spirit can not escape its doom, and will not have experienced even then the first pangs of its sufferings. Is it strange that men went wild with this dreadful belief? Ignorant men, who feared the unseen, intangible spirits of the air more than the accumulated tortures that human ruler might inflict, saw in the priests who claimed the power to control this intangible world, who held the keys of the Great Unseen, the only hope of escape. How well that order has seized its vantage, and, fanning the flames of superstition, stifled reason and led poor Humanity over the quaking boglands and reeking marshes of myth-theology!

This life is nothing compared with that which is to come. Its most innocent pleasures are sins; for the body itself is sinful, and by sin man came into the world. Pressed down beneath the weight of universal disaster, the doctrine of Jesus was the wail of despair. Take no heed of the morrow. Live only for today. Give all to the poor. Resist not the tyrant wrong. This life is a vale of tears, and the eye that weeps most shall be the brightest in glory in the life which is to come. O Jesus, on thy cross, what infinite misery has come from this misconception of thy teachings! Men, believing that their immortal spirits were chained to sinful bodies, rushed in herds to the mountain cave or lonely desert, and, by fasting and thirst, by hair-cloth garments wearing through the flesh to the bone, by flagellation and daily crucifixion, sought to expiate the sins of the body, and enter the next life purified.

Believing in an immortal life, they sought to force their belief on others, and proselyte by sword and torture. Dogmatism grew rankly luxuriant in this hot-bed of ignorance and superstition. Humanity was bound to the wheel; and ingenuity exhausted its skill in demoniacal inventions whereby severer pangs might be evoked, that through physical suffering the spirit might gain purification. Poor humanity might well exclaim, "Blessed be oblivion to this curse of Immortality!"

Not to lead a happy and perfect life, but to avoid the pangs of hell, to escape the consequences of original sin, was the object to which all energies were directed. And there was obligation to propagate this belief until received by all the world. Out of this doctrine came centuries of persecution, such as the heathen world never dreamed of. If your relative or friend accepted what you regarded erroneous dogmas, which would send him to eternal torment would it not be plain duty for you to use every means to persuade and convince him, even if necessary, by force? For should you, in last extremity, destroy his body, what fleeting consequence, if you saved thereby his soul!

The savage, having killed his enemy, trembles at the thought that the spirit has escaped, and may work untold mischief. He sits down at the cannibal feast, that, by eating the body, he may absorb the spirit, and thus be doubly avenged, by blotting out his foe, by making his body and spirit a part of himself.

Noble and spotless lives have grown out of Christianity, as out of other systems of religion, as beautiful lilies grow out of the slime; but they grew in defiance of its teachings, which make this life of no value compared with the next. As all religions rest on the foundation of belief in a future life, so all the religious wars which have cursed mankind are referable to it; all persecutions; all the unutterable sufferings, physical and spiritual, which have made the centuries one long night of agony. It has blotted the star of hope from the heavens, and filled the vaulted darkness with the bitter wails of despair.

Humanity rolling onward in a vast river, to plunge over the crags of death into a bottomless pit of eternal agony, and the best that Christianity has offered, or can offer, is eternal psalm-singing to golden harps. "Saving souls" has been the theme of the Christian world for nearly two thousand years, and various have been the means employed. Dungeon, rack, the flames, social ostracism--how shall I find space to catalogue the endless names of methods which curdle the blood at bare mention! The cannibal, feasting on his foe, is engaged in the honorable effort of saving a soul, and the priestly torturer is doing the same. The Brunos were chained amid the fagots' flame, to save their souls and the souls of others led astray by their doctrines. Go down into the dimly lighted tribunal hall, where God's vicegerents sit in judgment. Before them stands one gone astray in belief. There is no argument of words. On the table is a little thimble with a screw at one side. The heretic places his fingers therein, and the judges turn the screws down into the tender nails. The compressed lips grow white, the veins knot on the temples, beaded sweat gathers on the brow, as slowly down pierces the relentless steel, until at last, human endurance yields, and the trembling lips gasp, "Dear Christ, I believe!" Then turn back the screws, ring the bells, and rejoice with great joy; for a soul is saved!

From that hall, go down a flight of stone steps to another in the bowels of the earth, where the walls are reeking with mold, and the lamp darkens in the foul vapor. Tread with care on the slippery floors, for the slime of years has gathered; and now we have reached a great stone, which we can turn back like a trap-door, and reach an opening. Lower your lamp, feebly burning in the fetid atmosphere. There are walls of stone, there is stone for a floor. It is like a jug without an outlet, except at the top. At the bottom is something moving, living! Hush! It moans and has speech! An iron ring wears the bleeding ankle to the bone, to the ring is a chain, and the other end of the chain is fastened to the floor. What monstrous crime has this man committed that he should thus suffer? Nothing, except he has thought for himself--is lost; and his judges are making the desperate attempt to save his soul!

Saving souls, not the life here, but that which is to come, has been the blight and curse of mankind. The doctrine of "one world at a time," and the present supreme, is a reaction against this essentially vicious dogma. Neither extreme may be true; for the truth is the "golden mean," which makes the future life a continuity of this, carrying forward all its ideals to full realization, and making the spiritual realm held in abeyance to as fixed and unchangeable laws as the material world.

By knowledge, man has been led out of the fogs to the highlands of free thought, and aroused from the nightmare of theology, which for ages held him in thraldom. Those were the ages when God and Christ were inwrought into the Constitution of the State, and the Holy Bible was the foundation of the law. Those were the ages of St. Bartholomew massacres, of autos-da-fe, of the rack and the fagot. Those were the ages when the day was darkened by the smoke of burning cities, and the fair fields gleamed white with the bones of the slain. Those were the ages when the whole Christian world engaged itself in saving souls!

A Jesus may suffer on the cross; not only one, but ten thousand may die, admirable in self-sacrifice and examples of firm adhesion to their sense of duty; but, for saving souls, their sacrifice is lost; for they suffer for a misconception of the plan of the world. Man has never been lost, and can not be lost, and hence can not be saved by the blood of one or ten thousand sacrifices.

If the future life is a continuity of this, then the perfection of religion is the making of this life perfect. Not by crucifixion of the body, not by suffering or disappointment, but by complete and harmonious culture, can this be accomplished.

THE NEW METHOD.--To solve the problem of immortality by the methods of Science, to bring it up from the marshlands of conjecture to the region of absolute knowledge, belongs to the present age and generation. It is a task they can and must accomplish. It has for so many ages been the fertile field of superstition, that it seems impossible to disentangle it from its unsatisfactory wrappings. The investigation must commence with the physical man as the basis of the spiritual, as through and by means of the body he is related to the physical world. He is the superlative being; the last, greatest and yet incomplete effort of creative energy. All departments of science gather around him as a center, and to have perfect knowledge of him is to comprehend the universe.

In the earliest ages; in the very childhood of the race, the momentous question was asked: What am I? The solution was felt to be fraught with momentous consequences not only in this life but the interminable future which was vaguely shadowed in the mind of savage man. The answers given became the foundations of the great religious systems of the world. The conjecture of untutored minds was received as the true system of causation, and growing hoary with age arrogated to itself infallible authority, and required implicit faith, and the exercise of reason, only, in making palatable the requirements of that faith. Conceived in an age when nature was an unknown realm, when science opened her mysteries to the understanding, and one by one, dogmas claiming infallibility were shown to be false, there of necessity was antagonism and conflict. I do not propose to enlarge on the theological aspect of this subject more than incidentally. That treatment has grown "stale, flat and unprofitable," for every drop of vital juice it contained has been extracted long ago. The interminable sects, wrangling over the dogmatic solution of this vital question of man's origin and destiny, arriving at nothing determinate, wrangling with each other and themselves, are not incentives to beguile the earnest truth-seeker to follow their paths. If metaphysical theology contained the germ of a truthful solution, satisfaction would have resulted ages ago, and the mind, reposing contented with the answer, would have employed its energies in other directions. Instead, there is restlessness, turmoil, conflict and indecision, and never has been an answer so broad and deep in Catholicity of truth as to meet the demand. If science fails also, it can not retrieve its failure by assumed infallibility. Its teachings are ever tentative and prophecies of final triumph, as the grandest study of mankind is man, the crowning work of science is the solution of this vexed question.

PHYSICAL MAN.--First, as most tangible and obvious in this investigation, is the physical man, the body, the temple of the psyche. The student, even when imbued with the doctrine of materialism, arises from the study of the physical machine with wonder and surprise akin to awe, declaring man to be fearfully and wonderfully made.

It is not surprising that we die, but that we live. The rupture of a nerve fiber, the obstruction of a valve, the momentary cessation of breath, the introduction of a mote at some vital point, brings this most complex structure to eternal rest. By what constant oversight, by what persistency of reparation is it preserved from ruin!

This physical man is an animal, amenable to the laws of animal growth. His body is the type of which theirs are imperfect copies. From two or three mineral substances his bones are crystalized, and articulated as the bones of all vertebrate animals, and over them the muscles are extended. From the amphioxus, too low in the scale of being to be called a fish; a being without organs, without a brain; little more than an elongated sack of gelatinous substance, through which a white line marks the position of the spinal cord and the future spinal axis; there is a slow and steady evolution to the perfected skeleton of man. His osseous structure is the type of all. The fin of the fish, the huge paddle of the whale, the cruel paw of the tiger, the hoof of the horse, the wing of the bird, and the wonderfully flexible hand of man, so exquisite in adaptations to be taken as an unqualified evidence of design, are all fashioned out of the same elementary bones, after one model. The change of form to meet the wants of their possessors, results from the relative enlargement or atrophy of one or more of these elements. When the fleshy envelope is stripped away, it is astonishing how alike these apparently divergent forms really are. In the whale the flesh unites the huge bones of the fingers and produces a broad, oar-like fin; in the tiger the nails become retractile talons; in the bird some of the fingers are atrophied, while others are elongated to support the feathers which are to offer resistance to the air in flight; in the horse the bones of the fingers are consolidated, and the united nails appear in the hoof.

If there exists such perfect similarity in the bony structure of man to the animal world, the muscular system for which it furnishes support offers the same likeness. Trace any muscle in the human body from its origin to its termination, mark the points where it seizes the bones, the function it performs, and then dissect the most obscure or disreputable member of the vertebrate kingdom, and you will find the same muscle performing the same function. The talons of the tiger are extended and flexed by muscles, similar to those which give flexibility to the human hand, and the same elements are traceable in the ponderous paddle of the whale.

More vital than the bony framework, or the muscles to which it gives support, is the nervous system, seemingly not only the central source of vital power, but the means of union and sympathetic relation of every cell and fiber of the entire body.

The brain has been aptly compared to a central telegraphic office, and the nerves to the extended wires, which hold in communication and direct relation all the organs, and from which the functions of each are directed.

The nervous system is the bridge which spans the chasm between matter and spirit, and the battle between Materialism and Spiritualism must be fought not only with brain, but in the province of brain. However we may regard the spiritual being as an independent entity, when we study this subject from the physical side, we are compelled to accept the intricate blending of the influence of the brain on the expression of that being, during its connection therewith. The issue directly stated is this: Does the brain yield mind as a result of organic changes in its cells and fibers, or is mind a manifestation through and by means of the brain of something beyond and superior?

It is admitted by profound thinkers that the brain and its functions is an unfathomed mystery, and that investigators must be content with what may be called secondary causes and effects. Phosphorus and sulphur may be essential for the activity of brain tissue, yet it is absurd to claim that a superabundance of these elements wrote an Iliad, or solved the problem of gravitation. It is not phosphorus, or carbon, or nitrogen, however vigorously oxidized, which pulsates in the emotions of friendship or love; that feels and thinks and knows; that recollects the past, anticipates the future, and reaches out in infinite aspirations for perfection.

The actions of thought on the brain, the effort compelling the body to serve the bidding of the spirit, may consume this element and many others, as the movement of an engine consumes the coal and wastes the steam; but the coal and the steam are only the means whereby mind impresses itself on matter.

The physicist studies the brain as one wholly unacquainted with an engine would study that machine, and mistaking it for a living being, might be supposed to do. He would observe its motion, and, weighing the coal consumed and the products of combustion, would say that they appeared in steam, which after propelling the piston was waste. The design of the engine, the effect of these combinations and this waste, this observer would claim to be the guiding intelligence. And he would further argue that so much coal in the grate, so much water in the boiler and there appears an equivalent of intelligence, and the waste may be predetermined by chemical formulae.

Until the threshold of the functional activity of the brain and the nervous system have been passed, conclusions should be modestly expressed.

If it be claimed that man is a natural being, originated and sustained by natural laws, that he came without miracle, then do we unite the margins of the human and animal kingdoms, and are satisfied with placing man at the head of the animal world? An interminable and unbroken series of beings extends in a gradual gradation downwards, until the organs by which the phenomena of life are manifested are lost one by one, the senses disappear, until we arrive at what has been aptly termed "protoplasm," not an organized form, but simply organizable matter, or matter from which organic forms can be produced.

If, in reviewing this chain of beings, slowly arising by constant evolution, we closely examine several of its consecutive links, we shall find that while each ascending link is apparently complete, yet it is only the germ out of which the next is evolved in superior forms. Each link is prophecy of future superiority. The fulfillment of one age can be traced until man appears as the last term in the physical series.

They who teach this doctrine of evolution, which is to life what the law of gravitation is to worlds, also teach that united with the doctrine of "conservation of force," the hope of immortality becomes a dream.

What a sham they make of creation! What a turmoil for no result! Infinite ages of progress and evolution, during which elemental matter, by force of inherent laws, sought to individualize itself and incarnate its forces in living beings; ages of struggle upwards from low to high, from sensitive to sentient, from sentient to intellectual, from zoophyte to man! And now, having accomplished this, and given man exquisite susceptibility of thought, of love, of affection; making him the last factor in the series, he is doomed to perish! What is gained by this travail of the ages? Would it not have been as well had the series stopped with the huge saurians of the primeval slime, or the mastodon and mammoth of the pre-historic times, as with the man. As each factor in the series prophecies future forms, so does man read in the same light, prophecy-forms beyond. They can not be in the line of greater physical perfection, for in the days of Greece and Rome, man was as perfect physically, as is seen by their sculptures, as to-day. Ages ago, this exceeding beauty was attained. It cannot be in the evolution of a being superior to man, for as in each lower animal imperfect organs or structures, or partially employed functions, are improvable and perfected by succeeding forms, in man the archetype is complete, and no partially developed organ indicates the possibility of future change.

Progress having arrived at its limits with the body, changes its direction, and appears in the advancement of mind. Death closes the career of individuality, and we live only in thoughts--our selfhood is absorbed in the ocean of being. Mankind perfects as a whole, and the sighed-for millenium is coming bye-and-bye.

Of what avail is it to us if future generations are wise and noble, if we pass into nonentity? Of what avail to them to be wise and noble, if life is only the fleeting hour? Not yet can we believe Nature to be such a sham--such a cruel failure. The spirit rebels against the supposition of its mortality. The body is its habiliment. Shall the coat be claimed to be the entire man? Shall the garments ignore the wearer?

This is the animal side of man. Physically composed of the same elements, and having passed through these innumerable changes, he is an epitome of the universe. As man was foreshadowed in remotest ages as the crowning type in the series of organic life, so man foreshadows superior excellence. Springing out of his physical perfectibility, arises a new world of spiritual wants and aspirations, unanswered and unanswerable in mortal life.

MAN A DUAL BEING.--While Theology, Brahminical, Buddhistical or Christian, teaches that man is an incarnate spirit, independent of the physical body, created by miracle, supported by a succession of miracles, and saved by a miracle from eternal death, material science, as at present taught by its leading exponents, wholly ignores his spiritual life, and declares him to be a physical being only. It is not my purpose to reconcile these conflicting views. Truths never require reconciliation. They never conflict; and if the results of two different methods of investigation are at variance, one or the other is in error, or both, perchance, and the only reconciliation is the elimination of that error. The egotisms of theology and the pride of science array their votaries in opposition, while the truth remains unquestioned in the unexplored middle ground. Man is neither a spirit nor a body; he is the intimate union of both. In and through his physical being, the spiritual nature is evolved from the forces of the elements and is expressed. There is somewhat more enduring than the resultants of chemical unions, action and reactions in his physical body. Beneath this organic construction is that which remains, to which it is the scaffolding which assists, while it conceals the development of the real edifice.

Paul, the most profound thinker of all the founders of Christianity, very forcibly and clearly expresses this duality when he makes the distinction between "the celestial body" and the "terrestrial." In mortal life these are united, and death is simply their separation. His disciples have grossly misunderstood and mistaught his explanation. The terrestrial body cannot inherit eternal life, which is the birthright of the celestial. Death is the severance of the cord which unites these bodies in the seemingly indivisible web of earth-life. The terrestrial returns to the elements from which it came; the celestial remains individualized. It is unusual for writers on science at the present day to quote the Bible in support of their theories; but no author before Paul's time or since has given a more complete philosophy of life, and a key wherewith to unlock the secrets of the grave.

DEFINITIONS.--The comparison of terms has led to the strangest processes of reasoning, and the classifications in which some writers delight, have served as a means of intellectual gymnastics, rather than data for clear reasoning. In the threefold division of body, soul and spirit, by using the two last terms, at times as meaning something essentially distinct, and at others, as synonymous with intelligence, and each other; and again making soul and body the same, a most admirable means for the jugglery of disputation is furnished, which has not been left unused, and by which the discussion of this subject has been befogged.

There is the physical body, and the spirit to which the manifestations of mind belong. The term soul has no meaning, except as synonymous with body or spirit, and hence is discarded in this discussion.

PRE-EXISTENCE.--It has been taught that the ego, the immortal part, is from God, and at death returns to God who gave it. The eternal existence in the past of spirits, is presupposed, and that they await the development of bodies for them to enter, and earth-life, therefore, to them is a probationary state. The history of this theory is of profound interest, as it is wrought into the tissue of received theology, and its beginning traced to the conjectures of primitive man. It ignores the rule of law, and makes the birth of every child a miracle. The ancient doctrine of re-incarnation, lately revived, meets the same objection. A spirit, perfect in its individuality, through a germ becomes clad in flesh. It does not do this because the mortal state is preferable; for the spirit constantly desires to escape from its thraldom. It is compelled by a direct mandate of God to undergo this metamorphosis as a punishment, and means of atonement. According to this view, the development of man becomes entirely different from that of animals. There is no law, order or unity of organic forms. Creation is an ever-enacting miracle. When this scheme is referred to fixed laws in the spirit realm, the known causes acting in the physical world are but transferred to the spiritual, where they at once pass beyond recognition.

It is needless to say that with such speculations, an explanation having any claim to scientific accuracy has nothing in common.

ORIGIN OF SPIRIT.--If there is an immortal spirit, whether its duration be eternal or measured by time, as we can not go beyond the realm of law--by which we mean the fixed order of causation--it must date its beginning with that of the body. The history of the development of the germ is a correspondence of that of the spirit. If the parents have immortal spirits as well as mortal bodies, then while their physical bodies support the corporeal being, their spiritual natures must in an equal measure support the spirit of the fetus, and the growth of its dual nature be similar, both receiving nourishment from the mother. The two forms mature together; one pervading and being the exact copy of the other.

OBJECTIONS.--As the processes of life and that lower order of intelligence known as instinct, are manifested in animals, identically the same as they are in man, and by the wonderful interrelationship existing between all the members of the animal world, from protozoa to man, what is true of one must be true of all, it follows that if it is necessary to evoke the aid of the spirit for the explanation of the phenomena connected with man, it is equally necessary in the case of animals. Granting this, the next step is to show the absurdity of the idea that all the infinitude of beings, from microbes to leviathans, have a life beyond the evening of their brief day. The issue is fairly stated, but the claim regarded as absurd is not made. All may have spirits, from the lowest to the highest, holding the same relations to the body in which it is gestated as the spirit of man holds to his physical form. That such should be the case is a necessity of the position taken by this work. It is not, however, held, nor is it necessary that it should be, that the spirit of animals is immortal, or exist after the death of the body. They have not attained the requisite development, which has been likened to an arch which requires the finish, by putting in place of the keystone before the staging on which it rests can be removed, leaving the arch permanent. If this staging is removed before the keystone is put in place, the entire structure falls in ruins. In man, the arch is completed. Yet, as the animal merges into man through intermediate forms--and the infant knows less than the perfect animal--the line of demarkation is drawn with difficulty. It is like the boundary between the hill and its valley: both meet somewhere; but no one can say where the valley begins and the hill ends. A certain degree of development is essential, below which spirit cannot exist independently of the physical body, and above which this is possible. Any theory which of necessity advocates the immortal life of animals as well as of man, fails by maintaining that which may readily be proved an absurdity. For if the intelligent dog or elephant have existence in the future, so may the fish, the mollusk, the monad, and even the speck of protoplasm, which loses itself in unorganic matter. This was put forth as an unanswerable objection to the immortality of the human spirit, for it was said one or the other horn of the dilemma must be taken; for as there is no break in the chain of beings, between man and animals, even to the monad, if a future life belongs to him, equally is it an inheritance of theirs; and if it be denied them, so must it be lost to him. In mental and spiritual attainment there is a gulf between man and the animal world, vastly broader and more profound than is required to give him the inheritance of immortality which is also theirs.

In time this gulf is as wide as from the present to several millions of years previous to the glacial period. Prof. Wallace is so astonished at the difference between the brain of the most savage man and the highest animal, that he declares the theory of evolution, which he was first to promulgate, while it accounts for all the forms of life, here fails, and that man stands alone, the creature of another creation. While he says that man "May even have lived in the miocene or eocene period, when not a single mammal was identical in form with any existing species," yet he does not place the origin of man at a sufficiently remote era in those receding aeons of time.

In the primitive human being, thought began its conquest of the world, and the man of to-day represents the accumulation of all experiences since his ancestors fought with cunning craft the huge megatherium, and disputed for supremacy of the tertiary forests with palaeotherium, and other monsters of that age.

In time, the gulf between him and the animal world is thus widened, and in size of brain, which measures as a psychic metre, the growth of the superior life, he is equally distant. It has been remarked that the brain of the savage was so much larger than the exigencies of his life demanded, that it was comparable to giving the wing of an eagle to a hedge sparrow, or the arm of a tiger to a mouse. Rightly read, this proves the vast duration of time during the differentiation of man from the animals below him. Psychic growth is marked by enlargement of brain, and as long ago as the earliest preserved geological traces of humanity are found, that organ had attained a size and form about equal to that of the present. Its attainments have become so great that it is difficult at present to compare its intelligent manifestations with the instinctive desires of animals. The brains of all the lower types in certain essentials of organic life are alike, but in the great lobes which, superimposed, mark the degrees of psychic life, the human being stand alone, and is human because of the mental qualities these lobes indicate.

A SPIRIT NOT NECESSARILY IMMORTAL.--It has been said by a writer whose sensitive mind had received supernatural light: "Supposing the laws governing our spiritual natures operate similarly to those governing our physical, we must naturally infer that the spiritual forms of all parts of life, may be by those laws interpreted. If the spirit of an animal has not intelligence to obey, and the spirit of man wilfully disobeys, will not the law eventually destroy such spirits? The sentient notion that all ignorant and vile spirits, without aspirations for anything that is good, who glory in wickedness and persist in the violation of law, will become perfected I regard as false, for such must go on in a career which ends in annihilation." This writer errs in the cause he assigns for the continuous individuality of spiritual beings. He places it on moral grounds, making it dependent on moral aspirations, character and desires. Rather is it dependent on development as an entirety. The human being, after a certain stage of mental growth, receives a charter to eternal life which it can not annul, bearing with it all its infinite consequences and responsibilities.

In the "Arcana," Vol. II., 1864, this subject is thus treated:

"A spirit is not necessarily immortal, but can become gradually extinguished, like a lamp burning for an indefinite time and then going out. Such is the condition of the lowest races of mankind. They exist after death; but with them there is no progress, no desire for the immortal state, and slowly, atom by atom, they are absorbed into the bosom of the universal spirit-essence as the spirit of the animal is immediately after death."

If it be asked at what age the spirit of man retains its identity, it may be said in reply, that no certain date can be given, for that varies with the development of the parents. Is the idiot immortal? The answer depends on the circumstances, the degree and cause of the idiocy. If the idiot is destitute of a ray of intelligence; if it is only a voiceless, thoughtless being, the inference is not cheering, and the possibilities are largely in favor of its absorption into the bosom of the universal spirit-substance.

A sensitive gave his testimony on this subject as it came under his observation while in a trance. Its value depends on the credence we give to the revelations received from that state. He said that while in the unconscious trance, or clairvoyant state, the dying animal and dying human being were both presented to him, and he saw the same processes go forward in both. The spirit of the animal floated above the dying body like a thin cloud; and while he was expecting it to take form and identity, it dissolved and disappeared, just as a cloud would do in a summer sky. The spirit of a human being arose like a cloud in the same manner, took form and identity, and became a counterpart of the body it had left. This is not a speculative belief, but demonstrative by the revelations of trance.

MUST NOT IMMORTALITY REACH INTO THE PAST AS WELL AS INTO THE FUTURE?--A far more potent objection is made by the Metaphysician. To him the preceding arguments that the spirit can not have existed prior to birth, and has a common, a cotemporary origin with the physical body, is fatal to its existence after death. He says: Whatever has a beginning must have an end; therefore, when it is asserted that the spirit of man is immortal, it follows that it must have always pre-existed; had an endless past. This is a startling objection and held to be unanswerable, except by the hypothesis of pre-existence and re-incarnation, which maintain that the spirit is an indestructible entity, constantly rehabilitating itself in forms of flesh; but this hypothesis is only a supposition made in the childhood of the race to meet a doubt and objection. In an age of accurate thought it seems an anachronism. If we accept the doctrine of evolution--and, as the immediate explanation of the phenomena of living beings, it is the only, and a complete explanation--then we must also receive as true the corollary that instinct and intelligence are evolved out of the transformations of living beings, and that individualized spirit, if there be such an entity, must be the last link in the vast organic series from which it has sprung into being. In other words, with an indeterminable future it has had a determinable past. If the spirit has existed for infinite time before its incarnation in this life, it has had infinite opportunity for progress, and, logically, should have attained perfection. Not only should, but must have become perfect. It is readily observed that the fact of its imperfection necessitates a beginning, and the degree of its imperfection shows the nearness or remoteness of its starting point. If it be held that this apparent imperfection is the resultant of the spirit's connection with matter, it must be remembered that the theory of pre-existence has for its object to account for the evils of this life, and perfected spiritual beings, such as all must be after an infinite past, would have no need of incarnation to attain purity or excellence already theirs; and should they enter physical bodies, as spirits, according to this doctrine, they would not be contaminated or degraded by their contact with earth and earth-life, but would glorify it.

With the physical form given to offspring by their parents is also given spiritual entity which lives after the decay of that body, an independent being, the center of multitudinous forces.

Is this visionary? Lately an eminent physician has claimed that under proper conditions physical life might be indefinitely prolonged, and man be able to live in the body forever. All that is essential is the preservation of the equilibrium between the forces of renovation and decay. If this could be maintained, life would be prolonged, perhaps to the end of time, and an immortal oak or lion be as possible as an immortal man; but with the gross forms of matter this can not be maintained. The forces of growth and renovation are in excess until the full tide of maturity is reached, and then decay is in excess. There is not enough material furnished to replace the waste of the body, and it wears out, when death must follow. It is then that a new entity becomes recognizable. The material has become spiritual. Such an immortality at best would be not only undesirable, but unendurable amidst the changing scenes and vicissitudes of material life. Only within the refined spiritual realm can we expect to find the perfection we seek. It is a new province, subject to new conditions and new laws. There is seemingly an impassable gulf between matter and spirit, yet we shall find it possible to throw an arch across. Nature loves such blank spaces; she loves the black bars in the spectrum as well as the light. Between the tadpole and the frog there is a chasm which, unless the change had been observed, would be deemed impossible. Between the caterpillar and the butterfly; the worm eating rough herbage and the gaudy winged creature floating like a wind-blown leaf from flower to flower, the contrast is even greater.

How shall we pass the abyss between matter and spirit? More correctly, how shall we look beyond the dead physical body to the individualized spirit, and account to the satisfaction of science for the maintenance of immortal individuality from the wreck of organization brought to its most perfected state? While the animal has a similar organization, in its way, and compared to its environment as perfect, why is it that the claim is made that the individuality of the animal is lost at death while that of man is preserved? These are all vital questions, and rest on the logical affirmation that whatever has a beginning must have an end. If man has a spirit, the objector affirms that animals, too, must have one. There is no sharp break in the series, and hence no stopping point from the highest to the lowest, and, consequently, the primitive amoeba, and protoplasmic cell must have an immortal spirit. This, by reductio ad absurdum, destroys the affirmation of the immortality of the highest as well as the lowest.

We may regard the physical body as the scaffolding, and when it fails, the incomplete arch of intelligence built thereon falls with it; but this arch becomes more and more perfect, until in man it is perfected; and when the physical platform by which it has been constructed falls at death, the arch remains. This is an illustration of the idea, and not produced as evidence. For this evidence we must consider the more abstruse doctrines of force and its relation to matter. If we go back to the beginning, to the primal chaos, we find visible matter and invisible force. We may take one step further and find force only, regarding matter as the form of its manifestation. This, however, is not an essential admission in this discussion.

This force is the first revealment of an intelligent, ever active, persistent energy, which pulsates through the universe. What lies back of it; from whence it springs, we may not know. It is unknown, though perhaps, not unknowable.

As we can only recognize Force as Motion, and motion only in connection with physical matter, our investigation must begin with the emergence of that Force as the moving energy of the cosmic world-vapor. In this expression with the primal elements, unconditioned, its tendency is to move in direct lines. This is illustrated in crystallization which may be called the first manifestation of life--the dynamic force of life. This force, which as seen in the formation and revolution of worlds, is vorticle; in the vegetable kingdom it becomes spiral, and more and more circular as it ascends through the animal kingdom to its higher forms, and in man becomes completely so. This statement will be better understood by the accompanying diagram.

[Illustration: Diagram of the Individualization of Force.]

The straight line a, represents primary force as manifested in the world-cloud, or nebulous vapor of the "beginning." It was this force that directed every atom to the common center of the cosmic mass. If its history be traced, it will be found that the motion of the atom starting on a straight line for the center is deflected by the resistance of the crowding atoms, and approaches the center by a parabolic curve. In other words, the cosmic cloud would form a vortex like a whirlpool, and the rotatory motion developed would, before the accumulation of any great mass at the center, prevent further aggregation; and the rotating belts would, after condensation into worlds, continue to revolve in spiral circles which, because of the masses not being homogenous, would correct their variations by spiral orbits which often reaching a minimum distance from the center, retrace themselves by the worlds traveling a spiral orbit that becomes constantly larger, until a maximum of distance had been gained. This explanation of planetary motions has really no connection with the present discussion, except as it illustrates the parallel between the circle gained by individualized masses, and the circle gained by individualized spirit.

The line of force directly acting, is the dynamic energy of matter. It passes into the world of life in an ascending spiral, that at each ascension, instead of completing itself, rises to a higher degree. The spirals at b represent the life of plants; and those at i animal life, now termed vital energy or vital force. There is incompleteness, and the force ever ascends to a higher form. At d the spiral becomes a circle. The evoluting or individualizing energy returns within its orbit, and instead of extending to higher forms, seeks the perfection of the human being. If, now, the inflowing forces represented by the dotted line c, be cut off, the individualization of the product of that force is complete. It stands alone. The orbit of the forces of its rotation is fixed by the indestructible. As in the planetary orbit, caused by an oscillation between extremes, there will be variations, but a constant return to the point of departure. The cosmic energy of force having ascended through this pathway becomes individualized, as at d, and death severing the bond at c, the spirit as the centerstance of force becomes as at e, entirely detached from the stream of living beings. The force that apparently had a beginning, at least such to our consciousness, has by the cumulative processes of life embodied all that is valuable, and is enabled to exist alone; returning forever within itself, maintaining a perfect equilibrium between the sentient intellectual and moral natures it has acquired. It is the focus of these. There is no end to the individualized force in this direction; in other words, spirit is immortal. It follows that vegetable and animal types along the spiral represent incompleteness to such an extent as to forbid existence after detachment from the impelling current. This can only be attained by development carried to a certain degree, below which the force must disappear with the organization which manifests it.

DEATH.--Death is the separation of the spirit and the physical body; and as the former carries with it all that enters into the individuality, the self-hood, there can be no change in that individuality. In the processes of evolution, death is as natural as birth--one is entrance into the earthly life; one departure from it to a higher sphere of activity. Ever is it as of old: The angel of the sepulchre is the angel of the resurrection.

AFTER DEATH.--The student calmly surveying the pathway of evolution, seeing constantly in one age the prophecy of ages that follow; reminded by every form of life, of a striving to realize an ideal, and in man, finally, as the highest work of creative energy, finds that ideal type of physical beauty, and adaptation to the demands of mind, realizes that short of this last crowning work the plan is incomplete, and a failure. The line of advance to man is direct and continuous. He is the perfect fruitage of the Tree of Life. Having reached the perfection of his physical form, progress changes in direction to the perfection of his intellectual and moral being. In this direction it is never completed during the brief years of mortal life; but transposed to an existence after death, the infinitude of years is equal to the infinite possible advancement; for as no one can fathom the centuries of the future, no one can fix the boundary lines circumscribing mental attainment. After death the celestial being holds fast to all that marked its individuality in earth-life--its loves, affections, desires, culture, attainments, its fears--to begin there where it leaves off here, with new environments and happier methods.

It will find belief the rags of the beggar, concealing the one bright reality, that immortal life is an inheritance, governed by laws as fixed as those of the physical world.

Beyond this, in earth life we can but darkly understand. We have words to convey ideas of things well known to us--of lights seen, sounds heard, of tastes, odors and sensations; but mortal senses have not experienced, can not experience, the sensations of this higher life, and so there are no words to convey the sensations or thoughts awakened.

True, there is a correspondence, such as Swedenborg attempted to express, but failed because of the limitations of language. He was, like every one who attempts this task, with ideas formed in the idiom of one language, attempting to express them in a foreign tongue, which has no suitable words. There are barbarous languages, with vocabularies of scarcely one thousand words, yet capable of expressing fully the thoughts of those who use them. It would be impossible to translate the complex thoughts of civilized man into such forms of speech, much less the impressions and thoughts of the celestial life.

If a butterfly, endowed with language to express the beauties of the broad summer landscape, the soft winds, the melting clouds, the fragrance and nectar of flowers, should return to the old bitter herbage, where its hairy, uncouth relatives were feeding on acrid leaves, and spreading its brilliant wings to catch the sunlight, should attempt to relate the wonders of the life that was its own, how little would they understand, how sadly would they misconstrue his meaning.

For them there has been no experience of wafting winds; no sensation of flying; nor of sweet nectar food, or perfume and brilliant color, and of these no words held in common could convey any meaning.

For the full knowledge of that higher life we must wait. And it is well: for to know earth-life in its completeness is enough, and more, for its short years. As this life is the vestibule to the next, so a true knowledge of it is of priceless value to advancement there, and its culture, its moral growth, its spiritual excellence, are treasures laid up in heaven, and this is all that the freed spirit can carry with it in its transition.

Personal Experience--Intelligence from the Sphere of Light.

It is difficult to prevent the discussion of Psychic questions from assuming more or less a religious aspect. The reason for this is that all systems of religion are based on Spiritual existence, and from views of that life, true or false, draw their vital sustenance. The moment it dawns upon the mind of an investigator, that in the facts and laws which come under his observation there are expressed forces unknown to the physicist; that beyond, dimly seen, there is an intimation of intelligent, yet impalpable beings, he is conscious of his own high destiny, and the necessity of conforming mortal life to it.

The inquiry of the student becomes the seed-bed for the propagation of religious thought. Herein this domain is unlike all others, for the outcome of research within its limits, is the last fruitage of Ethical Systems.

Imperfect understanding, as that of the savage, blindly feeling without comprehending, yields the rank growth of superstition; while scientific and philosophic investigation yield the most refined morality.

The preceding pages show the important part the sensitive holds in the manifestations and study of psychic phenomena. The true position of the psychic individual is not appreciated, even by those who have given the subject much attention.

While in the preceding discussions I have spoken in the impersonal mode, I wish to add my testimony from years of experience, as a sensitive. I do this because it forms a somewhat necessary preface to the narrative which follows.

The mass of mankind understand the delicacy of the conditions which go to make up the sensitive subject; of the acuteness with which the nervous system is strung; its keen susceptibility to pain and pleasure, about as well as the illiterate boor comprehends the chemical tension of the plate in the camera or the subtle ways of electricity. To be a sensitive is to have at times the light of heaven in the heart, and at others the darkness of despair. A thousand influences are always acting, and the brain of the sensitive receives them all, trembles to their vibrations, and finds resistance to them an effort most exhaustive of vitality.

In this state of tension, disagreeable objects, opposing words, or antagonisms which ordinarily would pass unfelt and unnoticed, strike with rude hand, and give excruciating torture. The presence of an object or person may be sufficient to antagonize or destroy all ethereal influences. I know of nothing that may be compared with the acute depression of the mind after such experiences, which corresponds to the preceding exaltation. While the sensitive is receiving a flood of inspiration he breaths an atmosphere of delight, and lives in an ideal world. Earth and its cares sink out of memory, and the mind is ennobled and purified. When the inspiration departs, the rosy light fades out of the spiritual vision, and the mortal eyes open to the cold, gray rays of earth-life. How drear and sordidly selfish, poor and unprofitable existence seems to him then.

After the flood of inspiration comes its ebb; the valley of despond, after the heights of Alpine splendor. Melancholy and depression of spiritual energy may produce physical disturbance, which runs its swift course to death. Recognizing these facts, the position of the sensitive can not be regarded as desirable, unless the laws of the sensitive state are well known, and the subject learns to protect himself against injurious and painful conditions; even if he does this unexpectedly, conditions will arise and confront him, for those who are his nearest and dearest friends know nothing about the acuteness of his feelings, and may unconsciously produce the very effects they seek to avoid.

The sensitive becomes painfully conscious of a double life, for the psychic is so different from the common state, that the mind receives impressions as from two distinct conditions of existence. One is physical, held in common with the brutes, with physical enjoyments and desires for eating, drinking, and the passions; the other is the psychical, which lives above and beyond the cares of life, and dwells in an ideal realm of purity. One is the night and the other the day. In order to dwell on earth these two lives must be united. The physical body has its imperative needs, which must be satisfied, as the just condition of spiritual growth. There is less imperative demand for spiritual sustenance. So soon as the body has been supplied, mental lethargy supervenes, and desires to tyrannize; physical life overlaps and conceals the spiritual, and men live the life of beasts. At other times the spiritual gains such complete ascendency that this world is forgotten in a blaze of ideality. An equilibrium between these states is the most desirable, but difficult to maintain.

Sensitiveness is a faculty common to mankind and capable of cultivation. Now that we have just entered the vestibule of the temple of Psychic Science, and are beginning to learn its principles we may hope for brilliant results. Nor will the duties of this life be neglected because of the approach to another.

To the belief that mortal life is all that can be attended to here, and "that the earth is wanted here, and not in the clouds," the celestial sense would reply: "We too want the earth here, and not in the clouds, but we want the clouds also." We want the clouds to distill the soft dew, and bear on their broad shoulders the life-giving rain for the grass and grain, to slake the thirst of the herds and flocks; we want the clouds to spread their protecting mantle over the fields against the scorching sun of summer; and we want them to bring the crystal snows to protect the fields in winter. We want the clouds to beautify the sky, and reflect in loveliness the rays of the rising and setting sun. Half the beauty of the world would be gone without the clouds, which lift the soul on wings of aspiration. We rejoice that there are clouds, and while the earth is good enough for the mortal man, in the clouds there is a grander reality. If it were otherwise, if the human heart were given its intense longings, its exquisite sensibility, its delicate cords responsive to every touch of feeling only to be torn and lacerated at the grave of the loved, we would scorn the pitiable earth, despise the sham called life, hate the force called love, and believe that there is neither benevolence, wisdom, nor intelligence in the Universe. It is the clouds that give value to the earth; without them it would only be a parched and thirsty desert. There are clouds, and by them the spirit is exalted to the contemplation of infinite realities.

Without the ever-present consciousness of eternal being, religion would be impossible, and there could be no ideal of excellence superior to the gratifications of the hour. But man feels the aspirations for a superior life, a soaring out of and above the physical senses; he feels the promptings of duty, of right, of justice and truth, outwrought from his innermost being. The pleasures of the time are cast away; selfishness yields to unselfishness; and the spirit, amid pain, apparent loss, and the scorn of its fellows, proves its kinship to the immutable and ideal. Such is the true spiritual life: The outgrowth of spiritual science, which makes morality a birthright, and its expression in character a consequence of obedience to the laws of its being.

Spiritual life is universal and infinite. It is the answer to our hopes, desires and abiding faith. Whence come they? They are the mutual expression of our inner natures. As the flower expands, its petals bending to the rays of the sun, so we turn to the spiritual sun, and only in the warmth of its invigorating rays expand into completeness. As the foulest slime of the sewer, when exposed to the light, casts down all stains, and sparkles in the crystal waves, so humanity in the light of spiritual truth is purified and freed from stains. Hope, faith, desire, the poetry of the present, are the prophecy of the future! Their voice proclaims the esoteric wisdom which is wiser than all books; for are not all books children of the mind? Has any thing ever been written that no one knew? As the mind is the receiver, so is it the radiator. It cannot receive what it has not the ability to throw out. It understands because it is the sum of all the elements and forces of the universe. It is akin to the titanic energies which hold the revolving suns and worlds in the hollow of their hands, and can read the ritual of the flashing stars.

Infinity it has never exhausted, it can never exhaust itself. Books are imperfect stutterings of its eternal consciousness. It is as superior to them as the master to his sketch, the sculptor to his clay, the builder to the engine that feebly embodies in brass and steel his ideas, which alone are perfect. We are immortal, and hope and desire tell us the wondrous tale of an unending future. We cannot cast aside its awful responsibilities, escape its duties, or be deprived of its grand possibilities. The very name, Immortality, carries with it the ideas of endless progress, justice, liberty, love, purity, holiness, power and beauty.

Those who have followed the line of thought in these pages will have no difficulty in admitting the possibility, at least on special occasions, of spirit communication. They, in fact, will recognize it as a necessity. If those who have passed through death's portals should return, they might find even the most sensitive unable to transmit their thoughts, except in a most rudimentary manner.

The following narrative is an attempt of a celestial being to convey by words a conception of its glorious life. While, in part, the sketch must be taken allegorically, mainly it is a true picture. The communication came from our mother, Jane A. Rood, and the remarkable facts connected with her death are correctly stated. I more minutely describe the entrance into that state wherein the message was received, because it illustrates the preceding discussions, and the communication emphasizes and makes plain many points which have remained unapproachable.

The first stages were like sinking into peaceful slumber, and I felt the scenes of earth melt out of consciousness, while a strange exhilaration, peaceful and delightful, came over me. There were changing flashes of color, rivaling the rainbow, coming and going in receding circles, and then a misty brightness, out of which slowly came, as though the cloudiness were material in the hands of an artist, a form which I recognized as our mother's. A score or more of years had passed since the fateful hour when we were gathered around her couch, too distressed to weep, and awed by the presence of the silent messenger. Wasted by serious sickness, she was at last free from pain, and a smile of joy came over her pale face when she knew it was soon to be over. We thought her dead, for her eyes closed and her breath ceased, when she repeated with a voice sweet as music:

"Bright spirits await to welcome me home, To that blissful region where you, too, may come; Weep not, for our parting is only to sight, Our spirits may still the more closely unite.

"Perform well each day the task which to you Is allotted, and murmur not if you must do What now seemeth hardship, for soon you will prove 'Tis labor of kindness, an action of love."

Then her eyes closed again, and her features changed into a glad smile. There was now no mistaking the signs, and we went to our appointed tasks, feeling that it would be sacrilege to weep in the presence of such a triumph over death. We felt that we had been permitted to catch a glimpse of an unseen reality. As travelers in mountain regions are delighted after the valley is wrapped in twilight by glimpses of the crest of some tall mountain catching the rays of the sun, and reflecting its glory, so to us it seemed that the departing spirit had caught a glimpse of the light of its new life, and reflected a smile on the face of the body it was leaving.

How beautiful she was with the graces of youth, and the complete and perfected charms of maturity. No wrinkles were on her brow, no marks of care, anxiety or pain; she was ideal in excellence.

What has happened to you, mother? How are you the same and yet not the same?

The response: I have returned to my youth, and have brought my experience with me. I scarcely realize how many years have passed. Twenty-five, do you say? It seems to me not as many days; and yet, let me recount. There has been a flood of events, and my recollection of the last time you saw me has grown dim. We count not time by years, but by accomplishments; by what we do and gain in thought. I am pained by the memory of the olden time. You say it was twenty-five years or more ago! As I come again in contact with earth, my sickness and sufferings are recalled. How weary and worn I became! How I longed for the end! The love you all bore me and my love for you was the only cord which bound me to life, and as I approached the end I forgot even that. How much I suffered that day I cannot tell, but at last I was at peace. The terrible struggle between flesh and spirit was done, and the latter rested. I thought I would sleep, and yet it was not sleep. It was a repose of all living functions, and yet my mind was in full activity. For a time I heard all that was said by those who were in the room; but soon I became so absorbed in the thoughts which flowed on my mind that I lost consciousness of everything else. Oh! it was such a delicious sense of comfort and of rest! I was so very weary; I had been so tortured by pain that to be free was indescribable happiness. I had heard them say I was dying, and I expected the dread moment with foreboding. It surely must soon come, yet I thought I had not reached it. The darkness began to lighten, and I thought the morn was breaking. An intense thrill of delight filled my being, and the light grew stronger. I continued to rest, and a new strength came to me. I am getting well again, I thought, and, perhaps, when the morning comes I shall surprise my friends and children by at once arising from my couch. The light streamed in with a soft and a refreshing warmth. There were no walls to prevent its passage. I was floating in a cloud of light, borne gently and softly as a weary child on its mother's breast. Then out of the light, as though it had formed into shape and substance, I saw three friends, long since dead, and my own blessed mother. To meet them did not appear strange to me, yet I knew they were not of earth. When they came around me, taking my hands in theirs, and caressing my forehead, I was surprised at their beauty, and the sweetness of their expression. They read my thoughts, and answered:

"Yes, truly we are of the dead; and you will find that dying means to live."

"I thought I was dying; they told me so," I said, laughing at the absurdity. "But I have become well, never so well since a child. It is a joy to breathe and feel the fresh life come coursing through my veins. But why do you smile?" I asked. They replied: "Do you not know that your new life means death? How much you have to learn, dear sister."

"Yes, I have everything to learn; my life has been full of cares."

"They have been for others," was replied. "And such are treasures in heaven. For us to learn is not labor. If we bring ourselves into the proper condition of receptivity, knowledge flows into our minds. There is no effort, no wearisome study. We may know all that the highest intelligence knows if we are in the right condition."

"I must bring myself at once into that condition," I replied, "for there is need."

"Be not in haste, our sister," said they gently; "there is time, and you must have repose. The pain you have endured reflects on your spirit, and you have not yet recovered."

"I infer from your words that I have met the change I so feared," I said again, smiling at the absurdity of the idea. "When did I pass the limits of earth life, and why do I lose sight of my friends?"

"You need have no more dread," replied my darling mother. "You do not see them because we are far away from them. It would not be well for you to remain and witness their sorrow. We have taken you away, that you may first recover and grow strong."

As I felt the swift motion, which I had not before observed, for it had been to me the gentle rock of sustaining arms, I asked: "Am I to be taken away so far I can not return?"

"Fear not, child," she replied in her old way, "fear not, for whatever we justly demand is granted to us. The craving of the heart is not left unanswered. Presently it will all be made plain to you."

We were drawn onward as by the tide of a great river, and I saw countless others coming and going, as though on swift errands. Then we paused on an eminence, overlooking a sea of amethyst on our right, and a vast plain on our left. The sky was softest purple, and the light fell with indescribable mellowness over all--there was happiness in the air, and those we greeted were radiant. No words can describe what I saw, or my rapidly changing emotions. There is nothing on earth with which to compare the landscape. The softest earthly colors are opaque in comparison, and the clearest sky a murky cloud. Overcome, I wept for joy, and my companions wept with me.

"Oh!" exclaimed one, "how sweet to know that this is the reality; no more doubts, nor forebodings; no more fears, nor distress; a life that of itself is the highest pleasure, and yields us heaven."

I started at the word, for it recalled a tide of beliefs: "Heaven! When are we to go there? Where is it and what must we do to go there?"

"Be not impatient, dear sister; we are in heaven already. Where happiness is, there is heaven. Heaven is activity. It is the deed of kindness, the pure loving thought that makes heavens."

"What is its first principle?" I queried, "for I am weak and undeserving."

"Doing for others is the full measure of its law. This is the angel code from which every trace of selfishness has been weeded out. To do for others brings gain. The pure and noble angels bending from their spheres of light, labor for others in self-forgetfulness. When man so far forgets his selfishness as to sacrifice himself for others, he exalts himself in angel-life. To work for self is no better nor worse than the brute world, from worm to elephant, and is devoid of immortal gain."

How delighted I was at these words. The dross of the world was rapidly disappearing. The sphere of my earthly labor, which to me seemed so narrow, widened. I had been sympathetic with those who suffered, and to those weaker than myself I had given a helping hand. Little things of no account at the time, so humble and narrow had been my life, now had a new meaning.

My companions smiled as they read my thoughts, and one responded: "Dear sister, your weakness was your strength. It will be no effort for you to do as you have always done. They who can be unselfish under the coarse influences of earthly life, how grand must be their career under the purer conditions which here prevail."

As we conversed there came one from another group, tall, beautiful and radiant with light, and with his companion more exquisitely beautiful than himself. They invited us, and we went to their abode. "How beautiful you are," I exclaimed involuntarily to her.

"I am glad;" she replied, "for to be truly beautiful means that the thoughts are right and true, for they mold the features and through them gain expression; but it requires time, a great length of time."

"How long have you been here?" I ventured to ask.

"Many hundred years. I scarcely know how long."

"And you grow not old here?"

"We grow not old. The spirit knows not age. It is not limited by duration. It is an eternal now, concentrating the past and awaiting the future."

I had not seen myself since the change. I put my hand to my face; it was smooth and unwrinkled. A happy ripple of laughter came from my companions. He who had come for us said: "Dear sister, you left those with your body. The pure spirit has not the wrinkles of care or of age."

I looked at him as he spoke and my attention was called to his robe. I had not thought of this subject before. I had been so eagerly watching the faces of my companions, I had not thought of their garments, or of my own. What a change! What was this raiment? I can not describe it. It was a drapery as of a cloud, and its color depended on the spiritual condition of the wearer. I was glad that mine was azure, for that was the color of my companion's, and thus I knew I was like them. What was it? A cloud or woven light? It fell around me soft and warm, and with a luxurious coolness contrasting with the burning of the fever I had so recently escaped. How different from the roughness of the old garments was this fleecy robe, glinting and reflecting the light.

As we conversed, there came a spirit, who paused in front of us, dark and sullen. His raiment was sombre and grim, like his thoughts. "Can you tell me where heaven is?" he grumbled, "I paid a preacher to gain it for me, and now having lost all else, I want that."

"Poor brother," replied the elder, "you search for what you can never find outside of yourself."

"You are a deceiver!" he muttered as he fled away.

The elder brother gazed after him sadly, and turning said: "On earth he was a miser, and who can count the years before his regeneration? He sought wealth, trusting to others his religious and moral culture. The recording angel has written against his name not one charity, not one unselfish deed. He now must wander in self-torment, seeking and finding not."

"Was he of consequence on earth?" I asked, for he was proud and haughty in his degradation.

"Thousands trembled at his beck, for he had made them dependents and slaves. He had vast riches, houses and lands, mortgages and deeds. He was wise in getting wealth; but here mortgages and deeds are unknown, and he becomes the least in the kingdom; morally idiotic, mentally dwarfed, and a pitiable object of our compassion."

"How long before he will gain the light?"

"Ah! who but God can tell!" sighed my instructor. "Who can tell? Centuries may go by. He must first learn to ask; first learn humility and his mistakes. Then some kind angels will attempt his education. They will lead him out of his mental selfishness, and he will begin as a child in the old life. His task will be difficult because he can not enter the sphere of receptivity, as we are able to do, and thus absorb knowledge from others. His nature must first change, and complete regeneration be accomplished."

The coming of this pitiable one brought a wave of sadness over us, but it passed, and the sun was more gladsome after breaking from the clouds. I had rested in delightful sleep; I do not know how often, and the old life was like a dream. It was not possible I had been sick, for I was so strong, so gladsome in my strength, and activity was a delight. My mind broadened. Contact with my companions gave me enlarged ideas. To think was to learn; to wish was to know. I was able to look beyond the effect to the cause. I could read the law in the result. Every day brought grander views, and my mental horizon expanded. Even in this larger growth I found rest. The faculties, dwarfed and starved in the old time, called for activity. The weariness of the body I was leaving behind me. How lovingly my companions would surround me with conditions of repose. How they gave me fullness of life, and drew to me those who would reveal the knowledge it was my desire to learn!

Then suddenly one evening I felt an earthward impulse. What power drew me thitherward?

"Is our sister disturbed?" asked my gentle companion.

"Oh! so disturbed! I have been selfish in my new joy, and how could I have been so forgetful; so unnatural? My husband and babe; my son and daughter weeping; and I have not thought of them!"

I wept, and my companion folded her arm around me and gently said: "You have been under our control, and are not responsible. To have been subject to the griefs of those you left, would have been painful and useless. You are now able to bear a full knowledge, you feel that of your family and friends. I will go with you, and you will find what I tell you is true, and you will bless us for our thoughtfulness."

We were poised, as it were, over a promontory beyond which the earth hung in space, as the full moon in a summer sky. Beyond were the stars. I was aghast at the journey, and fearful of the abyss which seemed deep as infinitude. While I trembled it was passed. I was in my old home. A great flood of human memories came over me. How I loved the dear familiar walls, the chairs, the glowing fire and, more than all, the family group. My husband sitting with his head bowed in his hand, my daughter performing the tasks that had been mine; my little boy and girl at play; the babe asleep. There were tears in my eyes as I turned to my companion for strength to bear: Did I not leave my body? Was there not a funeral? Why is it so quiet if I have not truly passed the ordeal?

"Listen," said my companion, supporting me. "Listen. It was in October when you passed away. The bright foliage of the trees, then burning in scarlet and gold, had been blown away by the blasts of winter, and the snow covered the earth with its icy shroud. All you think of has been done. It is finished. Were you to go to the churchyard you would find a mound by the side of relatives gone before."

It was so unreal and absurd that I was bewildered, and laughed at my misunderstanding, and wept the next moment when I saw my family. I went to my husband and placed my hand on his head and called him by name. I called with all my strength to learn that my lips gave no sound to his ear, and that my touch was imperceptible. Then I turned to my daughter and threw my arms despairingly around her. She was singing a song we had sung together, and continued not heeding my embrace. Oh! how keen my grief when I found I was not known in my own old home. I, who had come from such a distance, my heart beating with love, found no response! My daughter finished her song, and her eyes filled with tears. I read her thoughts for they were of me. "Mother! Mother!" she was saying, and I responded. It was the call I had heard beyond the bars of heaven! I could not bear it, and my companion said as she again placed her arm around me:

"Come, my sister, you can do no good here. There is your child sleeping in its crib. It is cared for as by yourself. Kiss it, and we will go. Be assured whenever you are wanted here you will feel the desire."

I kissed my child. "Let me stay," I pleaded; "I want to sit in my old place, in that vacant chair. Then I will go."

"As you will; and I will endeavor to impress your daughter with some ray of sunshine."

She bent over my daughter, and by means I did not understand, her mind responded to the spirit's thoughts: "Your mother is with you, and retains the same affection for you she had in earth-life." With the influx of that thought a smile lit up her face, and turning to the organ, she sang, "Annie Laurie," a song we had often sung together. How thankful I was that one ray of sunlight gladdened her heart, and the memory of me was yet dear. I was grateful to the kind spirit who had assisted me, and then she said we must go, for the trial was too great for my strength.

"You must calm yourself," said my companion, "for this sorrow is without the least benefit. Believe it is for the best, and though the hour is dark, it will bring a perfect day."

"I can not prevent myself thinking of my children and my husband. My love for them is stronger than ever, and I could not have been persuaded to have left them for a day. Can I not, oh, good angel, remain with them? The fairest scene of your home is desolate compared to the earth!"

With tenderest compassion she said: "You are now in the earth-sphere and take on its conditions. You are seeing through earthly eyes, and affected by earthly ways. When we once leave this scene you will be no longer distressed. Willingly would I leave you. I have no right to force you away. I influence you as I think for your highest good. Here you are unrecognized, and are constantly troubled because you can not make yourself known, and by a reflection of the sorrow of your family. Whenever you can be of use to them you will receive the knowledge and can return. Now we had better go."

She placed her arm around me, and whether the earth sank away from us, or we flow from the earth, I was unable to tell. I have since learned how to traverse space by the force of will; but then I was ignorant of the method, and dependent on others. Now, when I desire to visit a place, or be with certain friends, the desire creates an attraction, which in spirit is the equivalent of magnetic attraction in the physical world.

When we again reached our spirit home our companions gathered around us, and I was soothed by the kind words of my mother. I felt condemned for my loss of interest in the earth-life which had so recently absorbed my mind, but it became like a dim dream, and ceased to trouble me. What if I should forget it entirely? I was appalled at the idea, and cried at the pang it gave.

"Do not fear, you will not forget, but after a time your affections will strengthen. Our sister has much to learn, and needlessly distresses herself."

The years passed, and I became accustomed to my new life, when a message came for me. The palpitating waves repeated, "Mother! mother! mother!" It was my youngest daughter, who had grown almost to womanhood. I knew by her cry that she was in mortal pain, and yielding to the attractions I was soon with her. She was motionless on a couch, surrounded by her relatives, and her cousin held her cold hand. "It is all over," they said, in tears.

"Can it be?" I eagerly asked. "Oh! can it be that the time has already come when I am to have one of my children with me? To have one of them who will know me, and converse with me? Oh! heavenly Father, I thank thee for this answer to my incessant prayer."

Then I looked closely and saw the great transition was approaching. I could not assist; I could only stand by her side and receive her. She seemed asleep, which I fully understood from my own experience. Slowly the spirit left the insensible body, and as I saw my spirit-daughter recovering her senses, I drew near and whispered, "Claribel." She opened wide her blue eyes, and I knew she saw me. I threw my arms around her, and wept for gladness. "Darling Claribel, do you not know me, your mother?"

"Dearest mama," she said with her old smile, "know you? Why, you are younger, but the same. Where have you been so long? We thought you dead?"

"Do you not know?" I asked, apprehensively.

"Know? What mean you?"

"Yes, I am what they call dead; and were you not likewise, you could not see me!"

"I dead?" she replied, with a laugh which recalled her childhood, throwing her arms gracefully over her head. "Look you, mama, how far from it I am. I have been wretchedly sick, and in such fiery pain; but it is over, and I am perfectly well."

We drew to one side, and she then turning saw the friends, weeping, and her body on the couch.

"Why do they weep?" she asked, "and who is that on the couch? I am confused, for it is like another self."

"They are weeping for your loss, and that form on the couch is yours."

"Am I to return to it? What am I to do, dear mother?"

"No, you will need it no more. Your life is hereafter with me and the angels."

"What mean you, mother, by saying you and I are dead?"

"That we are, my child. That is what people call dead."

"I do not understand," she replied musingly. Then going to her cousin's side, who was still holding her physical hand, she said, "Cousin Frank, what are you weeping for? Do you not see how well I am?"

He did not hear her words, and she spoke again, playfully patting his face. Then she saw that she was no longer able to be heard or felt, and threw herself into my arms, weeping violently. I soothed her as best I could, upbraiding myself with foolishly teaching her the ways of our life before she was able to receive. "My child," I said, "how glad I am to have you again with me. They will all come to us sooner or later. Now we will go to my home, for it is not well for you to remain. After a time you will be instructed in these mysteries."

I attempted to go, but found that although I could depart alone, I could not bear Claribel with me. I had not perfected myself sufficiently in the method, and her attraction was toward that spot alone. I prayed for the coming of a companion, and soon there came one to my aid. On either side we threw our arms around her, and then our wills bore her onward with us.

When we reached our home, and the loving companions came with welcome to Claribel, and she saw beauty and perfection everywhere, and felt how happy her coming had made me, tears trembled in her eyes as she said: "It is wonderful, mother, and I ought not to regret, but you know earth-life was sweet to me, and I had plans for the future."

"Yes, my child," I replied, "the days were too short, and your friends were devoted, but your plans are thwarted, yet you must know that all is well." Her towering air-castles had vanished; but soon she had far greater sources of happiness in the group of beautiful children she instructed.

* * * * *

I said I would not visit earth unless called, for the pain was greater than the pleasure. Even when called, I refused. "My husband," they said, "was about to wed again."

"It is well," I replied; "his is the rough, earth-life, hard to walk alone. If he so desires, I ought to be willing."

Yet I was not willing or I should have gone. It would have seemed strange, indeed, to have visited my old home, and found another in my place. It would have emphasized my death to me. Thinking the matter over, I said:

"No! I will not go. Let them be happy. I will not enter their sphere."

When, years after, the message came that he was soon to join me, I hastened to his side. When I reached him he had already nearly passed through the transition, and had regained his spiritual perceptions. As I came to him he at once knew me, and opened wide his arms to receive me. The years were blotted out. We were again to each other all that we had ever been. By intuition he knew that he had met the change, and the first words he said to me were:

"I am so glad the weary watch is over. I knew heaven was not so large I could not find you, but I did not expect so soon to meet you. It was like you to come, and I ought to have expected it."

"I heard your call," I replied, "and heaven is not so wide that I could not come. Now we must go, and I will take you to the most beautiful place you ever saw in dreams. You must not remain to witness the proceedings further."

He smiled at my words: "Why, you talk as if there was something terrible about death. It has been the most pleasant passage in my life. I have suffered a great deal in its approach, but when it came it brought only joy. When I saw you, I was so pleased, my clay-lips uttered my thoughts, the last words they ever gave. Now it is done, I must stay till it is over. I want to see how the relatives and friends act, and hear what they say. You know it will be strange to hear one's own funeral sermon."

As he would not go, I remained with him, and entering again into the earth-sphere, suffered from the contact. My husband was greatly interested in the ceremonies, and when they were over, he said:

"I am glad the old aching body has at last gone to its final rest. The children were grieved, and ought to know how they misunderstand. Perhaps I can tell them some time. Hearts do not break with grief, else mine would have broken. Come, now, my new-found wife, I will go where you wish."

I need not repeat the story of the journey or describe the meeting with our Claribel. Her father was of so happy a disposition, that he at once assimilated his surroundings, and became one with his companions.

"I have worked and struggled along," he said, "having little time to think, and I am as ignorant as a savage. I desire at once to commence gaining knowledge. How am I to proceed?"

We all laughed at his eagerness, and one said:

"There is time enough; you must first rest and recover strength."

"Rest! I was never stronger, and I am anxious for exertion. I feel mentally starved and crave thought food."

"You will find no difficult task. To desire is to have, and you will soon become in sympathy with the thought-atmosphere of our home."

Then one of our number, who was a poet, superior to us all, said he had had a singular and painful experience, and we demanded to hear it.

THE POET'S STORY.--I had been enthroned, and as I came up the pathway leading to this eminence, I met a boisterous throng of people. Strange faces they had, and yet they were familiar. I looked closely, and imagine my surprise when I found they belonged to me. They were the thoughts I had expressed in my earth-life. Some were dark, repulsive and inexpressibly ugly, while others were exquisitely beautiful. What a horde they were, and though some were pleasing, the greater proportion caused my cheeks to blush with shame.

"Father! father!" they called, rushing toward me.

"Away!" I cried. "I know you not!"

"Then we will follow you. We belong to you, and wherever you go we will go. We will not desert you."

"If this be so," I cried in despair, "then I am burdened beyond endurance, and immortality becomes a curse. If I must remain with this throng of tormentors, reminding me continually of early follies, then extinction is preferable."

What shall I do with this miscreant crowd, deformed and rude? I can not take them home to my companions. If these are embodiments of my earthly thoughts, how they would scorn me. If this is to be my retinue, then I must seek a new home where I am unknown. I must cast aside the companionship of this company. My punishment is terrible. I threw myself down in a paroxysm of grief and remorse. An angel came by, and pausing said:

"Would you escape from your thraldom?"

"Escape!" I cried. "Can I escape?"

"Do you not see that the most repulsive of these spectres are fashioned of the thoughts which are of yourself, recording your former vanity, pride, uncharity, selfishness and forgetfulness of others? See you that lovely being representing a deed of self-sacrifice?"

"Oh! that they were all like her!" I cried.

"Then listen. You must act in such a manner that the good will eclipse these shadows, when they will disappear."

Saying this he vanished, and I, reflecting, said that I would at once free myself from the dreadful following. Opportunely there came a spirit moaning past me. Her brother on earth was contemplating a horrible crime. He had determined to take the life of his mother in order to become possessed of her estate. The sister had vainly attempted to give a warning or to influence him, and in despair at her failure she had left them to their fate. I said to her:

"Come. I will go with you, and perhaps together we can prevent this crime."

She fervently expressed her gratitude as she conducted me to her mother's house. It was midnight when we arrived, as I saw in the dim lamplight by the tall clock, and the mother was sleeping.

"We can only watch," said my companion, "and if he should come, we can do nothing to save her."

"Do you not know that sometimes sleep unlocks the avenues of the spirit, and we can approach much nearer than in waking hours? When we thus come, people say they have dreamed."

I bent over the mother, her white locks fell from beneath her cap over the pillow, and there was something in the expression of her lips and cheeks reminding me of my own. I tested her sensitiveness and found that her mind responded. Then I willed these words:

"Edward intends to kill you with a knife. He will come into your room, and you must awake and charge him with the crime, and say to him that his sister came from heaven to tell you!"

She started as if by a blow, and with a horrified expression, she sprang upright.

"Who is here?" she cried. "Who spoke to me? I have had a fearful dream, so vivid that I thought it reality."

She sank again on the pillow, and there were light footsteps at the door, which slowly swung open, and the brother entered. The mother waited only a moment when she arose and addressed him in the words of her dream. It came so suddenly that he admitted his intentions, and pleaded for forgiveness. He had been made the victim of bad men, and if he could escape from them he might be saved. By nature he was not so bad, but he was weak.

Leaving them to each other, I started again for our home, my heart full of gladness, for I had followed the advice of the angel, and expected to thereby escape my companions. Judge of my surprise when on looking back, I saw a new form, more ugly than any of the others, the result of this act from which I had expected so much. As I gazed in despair, the angel came again, and with a smile said to me:

"It was a selfish act!"

"Selfish?" I asked.

"Aye; you had not the good of the woman or the salvation of the son or the happiness of the daughter at heart. You had only your own pleasure and gain. You would thereby relieve yourself of a burden. The world is ruined by such benevolence. You will have a long and weary road if you travel in that direction."

"I am a fool," I said, overwhelmed by my imbecility and want of spiritual understanding. "What can I do?" I implored.

"If I direct you, there will be no merit. You must determine for yourself."

As he spoke he vanished, and I sat down, resting like a weary pilgrim, overburdened. Then I saw a spirit coming rapidly toward me, and on approaching she hurriedly said:

"I am told you can influence mortals. My son is captain of a steamer, and having lost his course, is sailing directly on a rocky coast. Come and save not only him, but the hundreds of his slumbering passengers."

Without a moment's delay, I followed her, and came to the steamer. The gray of morning was flushing the sky, and the crests of heavily rolling seas gleamed in the cold light. Everything was quiet on deck, for the passengers were asleep, and nothing was heard but the steady pulsations of the engine. I looked beyond the bow, and saw the shore some distance away. It was a high promontory of black rocks, against which the surf was violently beating, and the ship was headed directly on the point where it was most violent. Whatever was to be done, must be done quickly. We went into the cabin where the captain sat with his head resting on his hands, between sleeping and waking. Could I impress him with his danger? I made the attempt and failed. I repeated several times with no better success. I became anxious, as the danger increased, for every pulsation of the engine brought the ship nearer to the rocks. The sleeping passengers, strong men, helpless women and children, how soon they would be called to face certain destruction. What agony the now quiet decks would witness! What waiting and hoping against hope there would be in hundreds of desolate homes! The contemplation unnerved me, and I was unfitted to exercise my skill in impressing thoughts on mortal brain. I was recalled by the voice of the mother:

"Can you not save my son?"

I confess that when the picture of agony I have sketched came to my mind, in my wish to prevent the catastrophe, all selfish considerations were forgotten, and I would unhesitatingly have given my existence for the safety of the ship, were it possible to have done so.

"I can do nothing unless I have aid," I replied, and with my whole strength I invoked our elder brother. Instantly he came. He understands the methods of impressing thought so perfectly that, as you know, he rarely fails. He placed his hand on the captain's head, and the thought he gave was:

"Ship ahoy, breakers ahead!"

The captain sprang to his feet, and rubbing his eyes in a bewildered manner, rushed on deck.

"Who hailed us?" he demanded of the drowsy watch.

"No one, sir; all is quiet."

"We were hailed," he said firmly, and gaining the bridge he sought to penetrate the darkness. He listened, and his face paled, for distinctly came the boom of the surf.

Swift were the commands, and the ship by a sharp curve doubled on her course, the rocky ledge being so near that a few revolutions more and there would have been no escape.

A great many of the passengers came up on deck, aroused by the unusual motion of the ship and the shouting of orders, and when they understood the peril they had so narrowly escaped, they embraced each other and cried for joy.

As I again sought our home, forgetful of everything but the benefit I had conferred by my journey, I glanced behind me, and saw a shining light, and afar off, in dim outline, the group of beings I so strongly desired to escape. Unconsciously I had performed an act that had placed a light between me and them. Rejoice with me, dear friends, I am enabled to be unselfish.

Then the elder said: "Our brother adds to his other good qualities, that of humility."

* * * * *

"The angel-life became more complete and perfect as year by year the loved ones came up from the shadows of earth, until our family circle was almost restored. After a time its old members will take their new places, and when my earth-friends are all here, there will be little attraction for me in the old life.

"It is yet new and strange, and cannot be described to mortal comprehension. Language itself must be spiritualized, and words given a new meaning.

"I have mingled tears of pity with those who have been bereft, at the same time knowing that their loss was gain to the departed ones.

"Activity is our happiness, and thinking right and doing our very best are the gateways to heaven. Earth-life is a joy only when the end is known. Here its infinite possibilities are realized. Not in a year or a century, but in the fullness of time can all this come. Weep, for it is human, when your loved ones pass the shadowy portals, remembering, however, that the spiritual sun on the other side will, by comparison, make your brightest day on earth a rayless night."

FROM EARTH TO THE INFINITE.

The mists are falling on the purple sea, The sun is sinking in the clouds aflame; For many a day the far receding sea And melting sky have seemed almost the same.

At first we met the bitter storm and cloud, With little sunshine on the darkling mere, The waves were high, the icy winds were loud; The days were dark, the nights were full of fear.

By every trial having gathered strength, And hopeful conquered every adverse gale, We now have reached a calmer sea at length, And with full hearts unbend the flowing sail.

Behind, the sinking sun reveals no shore Illumed with glory of his purple light; The land we left has passed forever more Beyond the reach of longing mortal sight.

A boundless sea on every side expands; We're drifting slowly toward the glowing east; In faith expecting yet more welcome lands, When toiling care, and mortal life have ceased.

Behold, it comes in robes of azure light! As sinks the sun behind the sullen waves, And on the pearly shore, enchanting sight, Are all the friends we thought within the grave.

And now, oh ship, your weary pinions fold, And rock to sleep upon the harbor's breast; This is the home, by faith our hearts foretold, Where we shall find activity and rest.

###

Printed in Great Britain
by Amazon